HIGHLAND WINTER

HIGHLAND WINTER

W. R. Mitchell

ROBERT HALE & COMPANY

© W. R. Mitchell 1973

First published in Great Britain 1973

ISBN 0 7091 3961 6

Robert Hale & Company
63 Old Brompton Road
London, S.W.7

For
MY PARENTS

PRINTED IN GREAT BRITAIN BY
CLARKE, DOBLE & BRENDON LTD.
PLYMOUTH

CONTENTS

8   CONTENTS

ILLUSTRATIONS

PICTURE CREDITS

Lea MacNally took the photographs of the ptarmigan,
fox and mountain hares. The remaining photographs are
by the author.

INTRODUCTION

When, as occasionally happened, it rained at Braemar there would be a belt of slush half way up the Cairnwell pass and powdery snow blowing like spume across the summit lengths of this main route from upper Deeside to the south. On the Cairnwell, 2,199 feet above sea-level, is the highest point reached by a classified road in Britain.

A Cairnwell outing in bleakest midwinter is less arduous than it may seem. The glens lie at about one thousand feet—or half way between sea-level and the summit of the road. Surgery by the road authority has straightened out the Devil's Elbow, which had been Scotland's most notorious zig-zag.

Further, the roadman's innate stubbornness in the face of difficulties keeps the road clear even when the ground on either side has become a white desert. The ploughs operate twenty four hours a day in snowtime for the benefit of local people and also the skiers who, staying in Glen Shee or Braemar—or converging here for the day from places scores of miles away—use the Cairnwell chairlifts.

Roadmen can do little about snow while it is still in the air. During my winter sojourn I drove in a Cairnwell 'white out'. Wind and snow, meeting at the top of the pass, blended and swirled densely. I slithered through a city-like murk with car headlights blazing and windscreen wipers flailing, praying quietly for deliverance from any vehicles that might be rashly driven in the opposite direction.

My spirits lifted when I drew to a halt on an ice-plated car park at the ski centre. Here, with melodiously jingling voices,

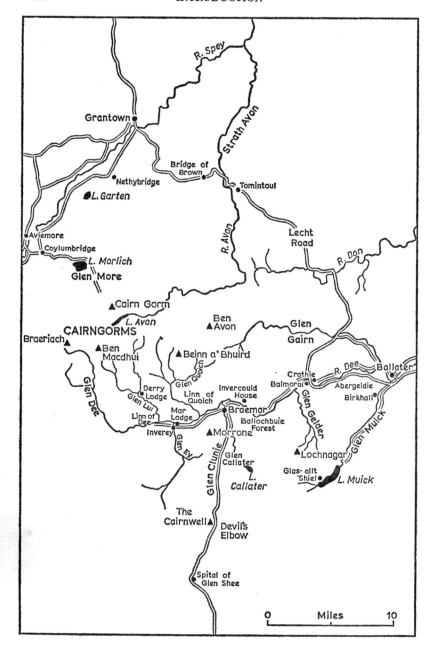

were snow buntings—bird refugees from the high Arctic—to whom wintry conditions are normal at any time of the year. The buntings shuffled about like so many sparrows. When their yellow-brown mandibles had closed on the last fragments of one batch of food they let the blustery wind carry them, via their pointed wings, to other heaps of castaway bread scraps.

On the morning of the 'white out' a four-wheel-drive vehicle foundered in a drift that overnight had arched itself between the road and the car park. By the look on the driver's face such a situation had not happened to his metal steed before. The vehicle was freed with difficulty and after much shuffling of gears.

A party of men from Tomintoul who were motoring to Perth had the Highland disregard for all but climatic excesses. I gathered that an inch or two of snow was normal. Tomintoul is reputedly the highest village in Scotland, and this little party had negotiated the Lecht—second highest classified road in Britain—when they could hardly distinguish where the high-way ended and the wild moorlands began.

A Highland winter has its moments. I ventured into Cairngorm mist at over three thousand feet above sea level, hearing—on this granite roof of Scotland—only the crunching of boots against frozen snow. For a while I stood in a silent, barren world, willing the mist to lift. But the mist refused to disperse and I retraced my steps, only to find that the world was less barren than I had supposed. A pack of ptarmigan, arctic-type grouse in winter white, went off in a flurry of feathers. When I broke clear of the cloying dampness I watched a small group of red stags go clatteringly away along a boulder slope. Here, in its sparse Highland setting, was the largest indigenous wild land mammal in Britain.

In retrospect, I should have been thankful that the air that day was still. The Cairngorms are frequently buffeted by winds of such strength that—as a roadman observed—"you can nearly see them". There can be rain on the wind—rain hurled at the walker with such force he has the impression that the weather clerk is desperate to complete the year's quota of about eighty inches as soon as possible.

One day a northerly wind gusted at up to 100 knots and plucked chairs from the Cairngorm lifts. The gale spared most of the shallow-rooting conifers that man has lately planted up the glens and across the lower slopes of the hills. There was a January night in 1953 when a few million pines, giving up their struggle with a gale, tumbled across each other like upreared dominoes that have been flicked to the ground. The damage, said a forester, was done by a "lazy wind". It was so lazy that it went through rather than round any objects in its path!

Foresters with young trees to nurture encourage them to root more deeply by lowering the water table through ditch draining. A danger period is when the conifers are about twenty years of age. Then, on nights when gales rampage through the district, foresters sleep uneasily and fear to look out at daybreak in case the wind has undertaken some savage pruning. I met a party of foresters whose job that day was to assess snow damage.

There is snow, of course. The heaviest falls on and around the Cairngorms occur towards the end of winter. When Southerners are rejoicing at the coming of spring the folk of the Highlands remain stoically attuned to winter.

A blizzard can be sharp and sudden. A day that dawns brightly will not necessarily be a good day; it begins to cloud over by noon, and then suddenly the snow dogs begin to howl. Or dawn can have an odd appearance, like an impressionist painting, and there is a long and steady slide into total greyness thickened by whirling snowflakes. In 'white out' conditions a walker has a demoralising experience. He looks—but sees nothing definite. He listens—and hears only a moaning wind. A blizzard may be composed of snow or pellets of ice.

When the high ground has been overburdened by snow, and the cornices are no longer stable, tons of snow break away from a hillside and roar into a glen with the speed and sound of an express train. It has been known for avalanches to overwhelm both men and beasts. Even the red deer, they that belong to the hills by the right of hundreds of generations, have been buried by cascading snow and perished.

Coroners listen sympathetically to eye-witness accounts of human tragedy on the hills. The worst mishap befell a school party. Six out of eight young people perished in 'white out' conditions on the Cairngorms, and the two that survived had amazing escapes, having spent two nights in the open. The young people had been making for the Curran bothy, which they did not see, though at one point they were only 400 yards away. They died under the stern gaze of Ben Macdhui.

Those who survive the savage Cairngorm blizzards mourn the dead and recall, in later days, the finer detail of the rescue attempts—the helicopters, painted red on noses and waists, that whirr in from Lossiemouth; the crackle and hiss of radio sets as voices communicate tinnily with each other; and the rescuers —stoic volunteers—who probe the deep snow with long rods made of aluminium.

Professor Gordon Manley—he who wrote of "the tingling clarity of a Highland dawn"—has pointed out that snowfalls tend to be heavier in the eastern Highlands than on areas further west. Deeside, indeed, is snowier than its close neighbour, Speyside.

Snow can lie on land above three thousand feet during 160 days of the year, with the cores of old drifts lasting the summer through. Snow actually falls on about fifty five days of the year. During the last really savage winter, that of 1962–3, upper Dee was clogged by snow for three months at a stretch.

I understand that Braemar holds Britain's all-time low in temperature, with minus 17 degrees on the Fahrenheit scale. That represents 49 degrees of frost. More frequently the temperature at night might plummet to around 20 degrees Fahrenheit, and then it is almost too painful to breathe. By day the feet crunch frozen snow, making a sound like that of a man champing cornflakes. The wild creatures that were astir by night are seen to have left tracks as crisp as new-minted coins. A walker notices where deer have scraped at snow to expose the vegetation beneath, and where they scattered their hard, dark-brown crotties. The snow was stained pale yellow where deer urinated. Hares, their hindlegs coming to ground in advance of their forelegs as they sped across the snow, have left tracks resembling a series of exclamation marks. But every creature has its recent history recorded by snow as informatively—to a trained eye—as if the details had been automatically fed into a computer and then disgorged as punched tape.

These are examples of some of the excesses of a Highland winter. Every winter is attended by some snow and ice and gales, and the nights are long. It is not the whole story. I recall times when the air was calm; when a hard, clear northern sunlight made the snowfields gleam. The air tasted as cool and fresh as wine brought straight up from a cellar.

In winter sunshine, the glens seem to burn with warm tints —with yellow and orange through to the chocolate brown of the ling, against which the wintering deer tone well. Scanning the riverside flats that lie to the west of Braemar I saw a golden hue imparted by the play of sunlight on wizened grasses. Those same flats later faded with a sense of mystery and at dusk scores, if not hundreds, of deer assembled here to graze. Two of the hungry animals darted across the road a few yards ahead of my car!

Winter sunlight has a clarity that astonishes a visitor from the south, where the atmosphere is frequently fugged by smoke. Highland sunlight cuts cleanly through the air with the intensity of a searchlight beam. This decisive light gives a startling degree of illumination to the moors and to the dark stands of Scots pine, particularly those gnarled veterans that carry on the spirit of the old Caledonian Forest. A line translated from an old Gaelic poem tells of "the blue height of a thousand pines", but one can also find contentment in taking a close look at a single tree which has the sunlight full upon it.

Winter sunlight can have enough warmth to melt snow on

the Cairngorms, to give the burns a voice. It is possible that one or two glaciers lingered on in the Cairngorms until as late as the seventeenth or eighteenth century, and visitors should still be able to have a snowball fight on Midsummer Day if they are prepared to walk in high places. Meltwater from the snowfields (such as those on Ben Macdhui, at 4,296 feet the second highest mountain in Britain) supports many a burn the summer through.

A Highland winter is rarely so severe that every glen is white for weeks on end. During my visit the snowline was at over one thousand feet; below that line the world was calm, sunny and serene for most of the time. There are winters when English conditions are more severe. Spending the winter of 1947 a little to the north of Deeside—admittedly near the sea, being on the shores of Cromarty Firth—I discovered through letters that the folk at home pitied me my plight. They were seeing snowdrifts almost at the height of telegraph poles, and presumed that Scotland had blizzards ten times worse. We in northern Scotland had some biting frosts—and a little snow; enough, indeed, to dust the nearest hills!

In upper Deeside I saw a sparkle on the young river, which was surging from its source 4,060 feet above sea level on Braeriach to Aberdeen, a distance of rather more than eighty miles. The Dee is a brisk river—too purposeful by far to create and maintain a large number of lochs or the most elegant ox-bows. In its greed for human life it has traditionally set itself an annual target of three people. When heavy rain and meltwater from snow had brought the river into furious flood, local people would say, "Blood-thirsty Dee / Each year needs three." Yet "bonny Don", a little to the north, "needs none".

There were few tourists in the region at the time of my visit, but weekend gaggles of brightly-clad skiers made their presence felt and heard. I was a freeman wandering on paths that criss-crossed a million acres. I trudged through the old lands of Mar, to the west of Braemar, where little seemed to have changed since Queen Victoria picnicked by the Linn of Dee or the Earl of Fife

B

instructed one of his men to hammer another mounted deer head on to the wall at Mar Lodge.

My excursions developed into wildlife extravaganzas. Over one thousand red deer were seen in an area where summer visitors sometimes despair of seeing even one. In summer the deer are high on the hills, but in winter they almost queue up to be observed, congregating at those places where they are regularly fed. Stags respond most favourably to such feeding. They are not tame. Winter rigours have induced them to suffer the near presence of man, who provides the bounty in his own interests—to secure heavier deer, with improved 'heads', or to reduce damage to the environment.

Roe deer were active, the males carrying horn in velvet. Some roe were seen skipping through the woods at half light after daytimes spent lying up in cover. Other roe had their 'forms' on the hills, where snow was packed hard. Entering Ballochbuie I watched capercaillie, the largest grouse in the world, and glimpsed a golden eagle soaring over a deer forest.

I found the tracks of foxes—lines of dots, like perforations on the faces of the hills. Once my nostrils received the sudden musky tang left by a disturbed fox. I watched mountain hares that were dressed in white for the winter; in some areas the population must have been at the density of one hare an acre. Hares lolloped in the half light from their hides among boulders and beside tufts of heather. Their chisel teeth set about the demolition of heather, which—according to Raymond Hewson, who watched mountain hares at length in Banffshire—forms 90 per cent of the winter diet. In thick snow the hare, like other hill vegetarians, takes anything that shows its head above the drifts!

I saw, indeed, a vast and simplified landscape with a variety of birds and beasts that once were common all over the country but now inhabit the remoter Highlands. In northern Scotland they have space and quietness. Few people disturb them in winter.

Queen Victoria, who commended Deeside to the world, called

her Balmoral estate "this dear paradise". Gibb and Hay, a writer and artist team who came to Deeside in 1884, were more perceptive. "Nature", they wrote, "is everywhere redolent of wonder, and replete with sober truth. In these we find abundant matter for observation and instruction."

1

ACROSS THE MOUNTH

The Highland Line must have passed beneath the wheels of my car near Blairgowrie, which lies about thirty miles south of Braemar. In between the two places lay the rough-and-tumble of The Mounth, or Munth as it was rendered, a name derived from the Gaelic *monadh*, meaning (I am told) mountain, heath or moorland. It is part of the slab of hill land known, rather vaguely—rarely in everyday speech—as the Grampians.

Near Blairgowrie I left the fat fields of the Scottish midland valley. In winter this seemingly endless, undulating and gently-wooded landscape holds flocks of grey geese that nested in the northlands. There are also wood-pigeons, in solemn battalions, clad drably in field grey.

Some of the fields had been ploughed, and with the shredding of the green grass a soil of reddish hue was exposed. A farmer said with candour that the land is not as fertile as it looks. It lacks sweetness.

Blairgowrie and Rattray (separated by a bridged river) once had the cloying tang of beef cattle about them in autumn. The burgh lay beside one of the drove roads along which cattle reared in the Highlands were moved on the hoof to trysts in the low country, and from here into England. Such traffic would benefit from the construction of a bridge across the river Ericht, but when the bridge was completed early in the eighteenth cen-

tury there was an outcry from the women who had ferried
travellers across the water, using clinker-built craft of vaguely
Viking origin known as cobles. Deeside was beginning to exert
a strong magnetism. In my haste to reach it I did not seek out a
savage reach of the river Ericht known as the Keith Falls where,
'tis said, a Covenanting leader, Donald Cargill, succeeded in
leaping across—a matter of eight feet—and left some dragoons
fuming on the near bank.

From Blairgowrie, 58 miles north of Perth, I motored on an
historic route which now has the prosaic name of A93. This
was a military road connecting Perth with Fort George at
Inverness, a distance of 164 miles. My route ran beside a wooded
glen, and among the trees were churring bands of titmice, with
attendant tree-creepers. It was pleasant to stop, switch off the
car engine, and watch a tree-creeper taking a corkscrew route
from a point a few feet above the ground to where the branches
of its chosen tree began to splay out. The bird moved restlessly,
its silvery underparts almost hidden by the brown of head and
mantle. In its speed and fussiness it resembled a mouse, but a
thin, needle-sharp bill probed the cracks and crannies of the tree
for food.

Nowhere, not even in wildest Scotland, do I travel without
being conscious that people have passed before me. It was
pleasant, during the run to Glen Shee, to bring back some of
those people in quick, imaginative dream sequences. I had a
comfortable seat in a car that moved effortlessly at forty miles an
hour. They travelled at much cost of time and effort, praying
devoutly for deliverance against the perils of the way.

The Cairnwell (more correctly, Cairnwall) is the longest, most
severe of three Mounth crossings now used by motorists. It also
lies far west of the others—the Slug Road from Stonehaven to
Banchory and the Cairn o' Mount from Fettercairn to Banchory.
Once there were thirteen recognised routes over The Mounth to
the valley of the Dee; they bcame higher, grander with the
blossoming of the hill range from east to west.

The sandals of early Christian missionaries who used the

Cairnwell route slapped a rough track that was nothing like as well-defined as the road that succeeded it. One of the Mounth ways was followed (according to tradition) by St Regulus bearing relics of St Andrew, to whom the church at Braemar is dedicated. When the saint reached Deeside he was introduced to the king of the Picts.

King Kenneth II, crossing in the tenth century, observed a deer drive in the Forest of Mar. It was hardly sport. In those days the deer were simply herded into conveniently confined places and slaughtered. On a June day in 1336, an English king, Edward III, traversed the Cairnwell and possibly had some pleasant recollections of the crossing. June is generally, to visitors, the most attractive part of a Highland year.

Southwards in the eighteenth century came a Jacobite army intent on reaching Perth, but their rebellion was abortive. Now a military presence was needed in the Highlands, and good roads were needed to maintain the show of force. The Cairnwell route was transformed by army engineers and soldier-workers between 1750 and 1754. They worked in areas that were unknown even to the majority of Lowland Scots, and among a people who must have resented their presence.

Military ways did benefit the Highland way of life by improving communications. Edward Burt, accountant to General Wade, who was the commander-in-chief in North Britain, observed that Lowland folk dreaded "the difficulties and dangers of travelling among the mountains; and when some extraordinary occasion has obliged any one of them to such a progress he has, generally speaking, made his testament before he set out, as though he were entering upon a long and dangerous sea voyage, wherein it was very doubtful if he should ever return".

Everyone who has set foot in the Highlands hears about General Wade, yet the engineer who devised the road between Blairgowrie and Braemar was G. Morrison. What he planned one hundred soldiers put into effect. These industrious men were members of a regiment of foot associated with Lord Viscount Bury. George Taylor, writing in 1776, approved of their work.

The military roads were kept in the best repair, "and so much has been done of late years to the other roads, by the Attention of the Nobility and Gentry, that Travelling is made thereby incredibly easy, expeditious and commodious; and such a Spirit of Improvement prevails throughout Scotland that we may venture to say a few years will complete all the Public Roads in that Part of the United Kingdom".

Horse-drawn coaches rumbled over the Cairnwell, and among them were *The Royal Highlander* and *The Earl of Aboyne*. Some of the traditional users of the route slunk to quieter tracks. They were the smugglers of whisky, contained in robust ankers draped from the stocky hill ponies.

Disraeli, crossing the Cairnwell on his way to see Queen Victoria at her autumn holiday home at Balmoral, was warmly clad for the journey. He was rejoicing that the day was "delicious" for travelling when he became ill and had to be attended by Sir William Jenner, the Queen's physician. Moaned the Prime Minister, "all is ascribed to my posting in an open carriage from Dunkeld to Balmoral."

Travelling by car, I was insulated from the world by metal and glass—which in some respects was a disadvantage. The countryside became sterner, with few trees, coarse grasses, outcropping rocks and streaks of snow on high ground. Grazing near the snowline were stocky cattle, beasts almost as tough and resilient to a Highland winter as the red deer with which I had at first confused them, for they were little more than black dots in the distance.

To my left appeared a wild and tously foretaste of what I expected the Highlands to be like. There was a tract of tufty heather, with grey boulders festooned with yellow lichen. This eastern part of Scotland grows the best heather—heather that thrives on the acidic ground in an area of moderate rainfall. The heather does not have to stand ankle-deep in water because the drainage is good. Where there are hollows, and water stagnates, one sees the bilious green of sphagnum.

Marshy ground near Dalrulzion was grassland, not moor.

Half a dozen whooper swans stood on the rich green turf, which
set them off to great advantage. Some of the swans slept; others
preened their plumage with their lemon and black bills. I stopped
the car, and the necks of the swans were raised as straight as
broomshafts. The birds began to converse, as though debating
among themselves whether or not to fly.

We tend to refer to whooper swans as 'winter visitors', imply-
ing that the birds have an off-season holiday here. Some swans
spend more of their lives 'wintering' in Scotland than occupying their Icelandic breeding grounds. The first of the whoopers
plane down in late September, and it is not until May that the
last bugling groups have taken off for the north. The range of
their southward spread depends partly on the severity of the
weather. They need unfrozen water. Strong family ties can be
observed in a large group of swans, with the young of the most
recent nesting season being clad, as yet, in pale-brown plumage.

The dry-land whoopers of Dalrulzion—and whoopers are,
indeed, more agile on land than the larger mute swans—were
seen to have black feet, a feature concealed as they swim. This
group lost interest in me. Heads were once again tucked under
expansive scapulars. I recall approaching other groups—of hearing the birds call softly to each other and then quickly moving,
facing the wind, slapping the water hard with their wings before
they became truly airborne. Circling high, the whooper swans
give trumpet-like calls. A small flock of a closely-related species,
the Bewick's swan, once enchanted me by calling rather like
Indian braves called as they circled a camp fire before going on
the warpath!

Snow fences of a style I had not seen before came into view.
They resembled badminton nets. Further on stood the heavier,
permanent snow fencing, set up well clear of the road with the
object of attracting the snow to itself and thus keeping the
tarmac clear of drifts. Where the perimeter of the road was
fenced by posts and strands of wire, the farmer had strewn hay
on the road verge. The sheep champed the hay after extending
their heads and necks between the fence's lower wires.

I left the last pieces of ploughland and entered stock-rearing country. Here were drystone walls, known as 'dykes' in Scotland, each composed of a comparatively small number of large, irregular blocks. Walls made without a dab of mortar were, before high labour costs, the most economical form of land boundary. A wall that is gapped can be repaired on the spot at no expense beyond the time used by the man engaged in the work. A waller worked in the tradition of true craftsmanship, by hand and eye, priding himself, as he fitted together the assortment of stones into a durable whole, that he did not pick up the same stone twice. His eyes assessed its worthiness for a certain position long before his hand went near it.

When I was in sight of the Spital of Glen Shee, and at about 1,000 feet above sea level, I could speculate on the curious name. A *spital* was a forerunner of a wayside inn, of religious significance and invariably set in a wild place. Early in the eighteenth century "there was a Hospital at Carnwall (called Shean-Spittal, or Old Hospital) wher ther is a road over the Grampian Hills".

I experienced my first Highland shiver. A chill set in with the sight of wintry hills ahead. A few months before I motored this way with open-mouthed admiration of its summer beauty. Everywhere were bold yellow splashes, the flowering broom, and the fields were verdant, thick with grass. Now, looking beyond a humped bridge and the church, I saw that Beinn Gulabin was capped by snow that extended downwards like a bridal veil. The cars that overtook me had skis strapped to their roof racks. The Spital had a Swiss flavour, derived from the modern style of building and the gay clothes worn by young people here for the winter sports. Highlanders, a dour folk who tended to be soberly clad, would have been staggered by the flamboyance of the modern taste.

Ponies, used for trekking, cropped the grasses, some of the animals being as white as the hilltops. The vegetation, low in protein, must have done little more than fill the ponies' bellies. Most of the cattle to be seen were black, though with some

Hereford characteristics. A sheep supplemented its diet by nibbling at a heap of road salt. There would be few sheep to be seen on Deeside at that time—and none in the well-fenced fields near Braemar where, a few months before, I had seen the ground polka-dotted with newly clipped sheep as white as Mary's lamb.

The hard country around the Cairnwell demanded hard, practical realistic inhabitants—men as unyielding as the hills and as tough as the weather, with womenfolk to support them who were not constantly yearning for towny delights. There must have been an underlying sternness to local life. Yet Glen Shee (from the Gaelic *sith*) means 'glen of the fairies'. Did the stern Highlanders believe in 'wee folk'? Local lore is also coloured by Fingalian romance. The Rev. Allan Stewart wrote about a fatal hunt on Beinn Gulabin during which Diarmid died, with a poisonous bristle from a wild boar piercing his heel.

Travellers before me had shivered when entering hill country, even in summer. John Taylor, who came this way early in the seventeenth century, spent a month in the Highlands. He crossed to Deeside by the Fir Mounth pass. The weather was cold and wet. "My teeth began to dance in my head with cold . . . and withall a most familiar mist embraced me round, that I could not see thrice my length any way; withall it yielded too friendly a dew, that it did moisten through all my clothes, where the old Proverb of a Scottish mist was verified in wetting me to the skin."

Glen Beag was a wedge between hill ranges. The road had an aversion to going straight and lay like a twisted ribbon between banks of heather. The peaks were mainly between two thousand and three thousand feet. Cairnwell, after which the pass is named, is not the highest, but rises to just over three thousand feet.

The sky held a patch of blue "as big as a patch on a Dutchman's trousers", as the haymakers on my native Pennines used to remark, knowing that the weather must improve. Elsewhere in the sky were massed clouds of half a dozen shades of grey. The car tyres slopped through slush and were soon crunching fresh snow. Gloomy and refrigerated, the approach to the Devil's Elbow had an arctic atmosphere. There was only one building, adorned by the mounted antlers of red deer.

Parking the car just off the road I stepped into a wind that had an edge like a knife blade. A vehicle drew up behind me, and from it stepped a stalker who had some 'slack time' on his hands. A white hare shoot, planned for that day, had been postponed because of inclement weather. He had culled the red deer hinds, a task usually carried out in December and January, though the open season for shooting hinds extends from October into February. The stalker was relaxing after some bitter days when he inched forward in snow to get within range of the hinds chosen for culling. When a hind is shot, it must be gralloched—gutted—and then lugged back to the pony or Land-Rover, a strenuous task.

The stalker, having experience of the solitude that leads to taciturnity, was keen to exercise his mind through a chat with a stranger. His lean frame was swaddled in the tweed that is a uniform on the Scottish hills. He was ultra-sensitive to the countryside around us. What had seemed to be a barren wilderness to me was, through the help of his eyes and ears, a setting in which a variety of birds and beasts could be seen struggling against the weather—and each other.

A cock grouse called, fifty yards away. The sound was quick, irritable, as the bird urged us to leave. The becking of grouse, one of the most familiar sounds on the hill, is uttered with a tone of voice that has a human quality and is frequently rendered, "go back, go back, go back." Richard Kearton, a gamekeeper's son who became a pioneer of wildlife photography and knew the Highlands well, told of a gamekeeper with a fretful wife who decided to leave her for good. He set off from his remote home shortly before dawn. At first light, the grouse began to call, "go back". He pondered a little, took their advice, and was back home shortly afterwards!

The grouse called again. I saw a bronze-brown bird with red wattles and feathered legs, sturdy denizen of the moor. The grouse peered at us from behind a tuft of ling. A red grouse is held captive on the heatherlands because of a considerable dependence on *Calluna* as food. I did not envy the birds their winter diet. In the breakdown of the tough fare they have the assistance of quartz grit that is taken into their crops and renewed from time to time.

A carrion crow drifted across the scene like a burnt fragment from a November bonfire—a big, bold, opportunist bird about which no dedicated gamekeeper or farmer can talk without becoming fiercely emotional. The stalker told of crows that work the moor like pointers, seeking grouse eggs or chicks. A farmer would relate that sheep, when rigged (lying helpless on their backs) often have a crow in attendance and the bird might pluck the sheep's eyes from its still living head. The same thing happens to weakly lambs in spring. It is pointless to suggest to these closely-involved countrymen that maybe only a small number of crows are filching eyes, and that they may have initially been attracted to the crofts by the afterbirth. Or to point out the value of crows as carrion-eaters—feathered 'dustmen'.

The wind moaned around a crag on which the snow lay like fine powder. A white bird alighted, and its point of impact was indicated by a trail of snow crystals streaming in the wind. Momentarily in view was a ptarmigan, a grouse of the tundral areas. This bird has three main moults a year, and the most spectacular of them is into a winter plumage of gleaming white.

Ptarmigan are customarily found above the 2,500-feet contour line, and the range extends to the very summit of the hills, over four thousand feet on the Cairngorms. Ptarmigan take over where the range of the red grouse peters out, where heatherland gives way to the barrens. When some ptarmigan drop lower down the hills in winter, the range of the two species may overlap, as happens by the Cairnwell Pass.

My view of the ptarmigan was unsatisfactory, but there was no mistaking the form of the bird, its absence of strong colour and the mode of flight. The stalker confirmed my identification.

Later, seeing a ptarmigan pictured in a book, revealed with great clarity, I could appreciate its winter beauty. There is some black on the tail feathers and (on the cock bird alone) a black stripe behind the eye.

Snow is an old enemy of the ptarmigan. It scratches snow away so that it can feed on the lichen, moss and heathy plants. It roosts away from the chilling blasts by excavating chambers in snow drifts—as do the mountain hare and red grouse. The ptarmigan plumage, especially thick, gives special insulation from the cold and this bird thrives where other species of bird would surely starve. Charles St John, writing last century, marvelled at its ability to live in austere country. "It is difficult to ascertain, indeed, what food the ptarmigan can find in sufficient quantities on the barren heights where they are found," he wrote.

As the snowfields begin to melt, cock ptarmigan are overswept by spring fever. They fight with each other over territory, and their hoarse croaking (at times even a belch) sounds over the chilled summits. I could not imagine a ptarmigan living away from its hilltops, but the stalker told me of a game fair held at Blair Drummond a few years ago. There were young ptarmigan on view—hatched, he believed, from eggs picked up on Lochnager.

Hilltops at great height are tolerable to this grouse of the high Arctic. The bird is so hardy, so accustomed to facing rough conditions, that a flush of warm sunlight in summer tends to send it scuttering to the nearest snowdrifts to cool off! Its chosen hills, scattered with rocks, sustaining a diminutive plant life that needs long roots to ensure a supply of moisture, stand out like islands. Here are the remnants of the type of tundral landscape which for a time covered the country in the wake of retreating ice. The ptarmigan was then a widespread species. If, as some believe, we are in an inter-glacial period, the species may yet come back into its own!

Sportsmen tended to ignore the ptarmigan. Writer after writer on sporting topics mentioned the difficulty of reaching them, and often during the sportsman's months the hills have grey sleet upon them (if they have not been blotted out by snow) or they are enveloped by mist. Men are considerably less hardy than the birds. Modern visitors easily reach ptarmigan country by using the chairlifts.

Basic elements, weather and available food, govern the ptarmigan population. In good times the birds are so numerous they become their own worst enemies. Stress factors and, eventually, food shortages, cause a cutback in numbers—and there is a slow recovery to another peak year.

Said the stalker, "Quite a lot of ptarmigan never come down the hill. They manage to survive, somehow. You notice about March that they are moulting, starting to go grey." We discussed the ebb and flow of life up and down the wintry hillside. "Nature never seems to allow any creature to relax," the stalker observed.

2

HIGHLAND TIGER

Highland tiger is a somewhat colourful name for the Scottish wild cat. I told the stalker that once I stood only four feet from a wild cat. He waited quietly, with courtesy, for an explanation and tried hard not to laugh when I added that I had been in a wildlife park.

The cat was a true Scot, born in Caithness, and it was certainly very wild. Having no alternative but to face me, it crouched with head low, ears trained backwards and mouth partly open, revealing the gleam of teeth. The white whiskers seemed to vibrate like a tuning fork.

There were few chances of seeing a wild cat on the hill, said the stalker. The species lived there and was more common than for many years; there might be a wild cat within half a mile of where we were standing. The new conifer plantations of the Forestry Commission offered cover, quietness and regular food. A wild cat took voles and mice and much else in the forest. The hill cat's fare included grouse and ptarmigan. "It prefers fresh meat to carrion, but condescends to eat carrion when little else is available."

Wild cats, I was told, operated mainly at night, when modern man was either watching television or sleeping. The stalker had seen wild cats, but not so often that he had lost his feeling of delight in their presence. He had also seen many dead wild cats —animals shot as they bolted or found after they had blundered into traps and snares set for foxes.

A cat on the hill, or in a forest ride, was not necessarily a wild cat—*Felis silvestris*, to which some romantics add the name *grampia*. Feral moggies were more numerous than ever, and they could look fierce and rough in their exile from the haunts of man. Undoubtedly there were cases where the domestics (of Egyptian origin) cross-bred with the wild strain, which is a distinguished and long-residing member of the British fauna.

That wild cats were once common on Deeside is testified by an organisation that operated between 1776 and 1786. It had the breathtaking title of "Association for the Destruction of Foxes and other Ravenous Beasts and Birds, and for the Preservation of Sheep, Game and Poultry, within the Parishes of Braemar, Crathie, Glenmuick, Tullick and Glengarden". Forty-four wild cats were accounted for.

By 1861, according to the Rev. James M. Crombie, "the wild cat is far from being common, thanks to the exertions of the gamekeepers who contrive to keep them down, and in all probability will soon succeed in extirpating them altogether". The stalker told me that one wild cat almost extirpated a friend of his who, having shot the beast, laid down his gun and advanced upon the 'corpse', which sprang up and clawed him about the face. The stalker told me that wild cat kits were dropped between April and August, "which is a longish season for litters".

I recalled at leisure the only Scottish wild cat I had seen alive —excepting the greyish blur that crossed my path when I walked just north of the Great Glen, being noted down as a 'probable' wild cat. The captive animal was forever in the view of those who went along to see it, and there were many. Its wild relations would be mainly active at dawn and dusk, tending to lie up by day and during wet weather, for no cat likes to have its hair draggled by sodden vegetation. This cat had a substantial roof over its head!

I saw a hefty male, a prize item in a collection of European mammals. In the next enclosure was a pair of foxes, the dog then tucked away in the shadows and the vixen lying motion-

c

less in a man-made den which she had not left since cubs were born several days before. A close proximity of wild cat and fox was appropriate, for the two species must see a lot of each other on a Scottish hill.

The wild cat lay placidly asleep, with a Cheshire-type smile on the broad grey face, but the head was flattish, the pelage thick (almost like tufts of fine wire) and the bushy tail that lay curled around the animal's stocky body was blunt-ended, banded with black—all good pointers to the purity of its breeding. It is said that the British sub-species of wild cat is darker, more boldly marked, than are its cousins on the Continent. Experts can argue about that as they will. Wild cats are found across Europe to the Caucasus.

The eyes of the captive cat flickered as I watched. I saw two brilliant flashes. Slightly irritated at being overlooked from close range, the animal was doubtless dreaming of the cool and gloom of late evening when, the visitors gone, it might slink un-observed into a larger enclosure to sharpen its claws against one of the tree branches reared up for it—or lie on a horizontal branch, when it could be as unmoving and inscrutable as the wood itself. This wild cat's food was carrion—small, dead mammals, complete with bone and fur, for it must have roughage as well as meat.

Few Britons have taken the time, trouble and superhuman patience to study the wild cat in the wild over prolonged periods. Continental research has tended to bear out much that was known to the Victorian sportsman, Charles St John. He wrote, many years ago, that "in hunting the most lonely and inaccessible ranges of rock and mountain, the wild cat is seldom seen during the day time; at night (like its domestic relative) he prowls far and wide, walking with the same deliberate step, making the same regular and even track, and hunting his game in the same tiger-like manner; and yet the difference between the two animals is perfectly clear, and visible to the commonest observer. The wild cat has a shorter and more bushy tail, stands higher on her legs in proportion to her size, and has a rounder and coarser look about the head." St John's cat changed its sex half way through the paragraph!

The owner of the cat kept in the wildlife park allowed me to approach it from the rear of its box, using the door through which its bedding was occasionally replaced and food was delivered. As we approached, with some shivering, because of the wild cat's reputation, I heard a fierce growling from beyond a wooden partition. The owner spoke to the animal as he slowly unlocked the door and swung it open. He used endearing words like "pussy". They seemed inappropriate when directed towards a Highland tiger.

The thought of the cat escaping from the box and finding its range restricted to the limited space between various doors was indeed chilling. Would it savagely lash out at us? When the moment came for me to look into the compartment I did so through a camera lens, thus protecting my face. Into view came the crouching cat, and it almost crackled with fury. When it shifted its position I was impressed by the rapid changes of emotion. There was a lack of sublety—just instant relaxation or instant fury, switching to and fro decisively, like a railway signal.

Drawing itself erect, but keeping the head fairly low and ears down, the wild cat hissed defiantly, using a threatening pose for a second time before departing through a hole behind it—the entrance to its larger compound, which I had initially failed to notice. My last sight was of a tail dangling, ringed by bold black stripes, as the cat prepared to spring for freedom.

My views of the wildcat were obtained without effort. I therefore did not value them greatly. Charles St John, who knew the free-ranging animal well, wrote that "in the hanging birchwoods that border some of the Highland streams and lochs, the wild cat is still not uncommon. I have heard their wild and unearthly cry echo far in the quiet night as they answer and call to each other. I do not know a more harsh and unpleasant cry than that of the wild cat, or one more likely to be the origin of superstitious fears in the mind of an ignorant Highlander."

3

DEVIL'S ELBOW

The final approach to the summit of the Cairnwell Pass developed into a long drag, with the road wide, edged by curbstones. Successive signs indicated gradients of 1 in 10, 1 in 9 and finally 1 in 7. Meltwater from snow rippled across the road.

I parked at an unnerving angle to survey some 'black ground' through binoculars. Several mountain hares were visible, in varying degrees of whiteness. Not all the animals of this species go white as illustrations of them in books lead one to suppose. The majority, indeed, have a patchy appearance.

A red grouse alighted, giving me its rough position, and I sought it out, looking for the scarlet of the wattles. Man acquired an unfair advantage over his fellow creatures when he invented telescopes and binoculars and could watch them clearly from afar.

The shock waves of my lingering presence upset seven red stags, and the animals moved slowly, diagonally, across a hill face about a quarter of a mile away. They were uneasy during their retreat over patches of heather during which they left their slots deep-printed in drifts of snow. Their winter coats were like thick grey-brown blankets.

Even at a time of disquiet the stags could not resist feeding, briefly cropping the coarse grasses and the ling, which were low in food value. In summer they would satisfy their appetites in a fraction of the time needed in winter.

A Scottish hill stag is on short rations for about a third of the year, and must feed incessantly to maintain some sort of condition. In contrast are the larger stags cossetted in English parks, where they are fed regularly, attaining twice the weight of the stags I now had in view. The best Continental animals are heavier still. All are red deer, members of a species which—perhaps more conspicuously than any other—reflects by its size the nature of the ground on which it lives.

My gaze lingered on the stags. The best of them would weigh around 15 stone 'clean', had reached its prime at between six and eight years old and, with luck, might live to be fifteen. As with humans, the female deer tends to live rather longer than the male. A good red hind makes the scales dip at around 9 stone.

The Highland red lives on the poorest ground in Britain, yet not only does it survive—it thrives, rapidly converting vegetation into venison and in summer grazing the high corries that otherwise would have no economic value to man. It is the same with sheep. Without his flocks man would not be able to get a cash profit from a considerable area of hill land.

Some naturalists would like to see fewer sheep on the hills, and a stiff culling programme is needed to keep the deer population at an acceptable level. The signs of overstocking by deer are clear to see in the extensive browsing of a shrub like juniper and in the fact that the ground beneath the pines is devoid of saplings when naturally there would be a liberal covering.

Deer are fed in winter by many estates, which now place protein and mineral licks on the hill. The stags are most inclined to accept the hay, potatoes and special nuts distributed at set points. Hinds, which normally stay apart from the stags except during the rutting season, are still jittery after the culling season, though arguably they should be the animals to receive first consideration as the mothers of the next generation. Within them, through the winter, develop the calves they will drop in spring.

William Scrope, who in the mid-nineteenth century popularized sport with deer by writing *The Art of Deer-Stalking*, gave us a vivid word picture of the wintering stag.

He does not by choice subsist on coarse food, but eats close, like a sheep. With his body weakened and wasted during the rutting season in the autumn, exposed to constant anxiety and irritation, and engaged in continual combats, he feels all the rigours of winter approaching before he has time to recruit his strength.

The snowstorm comes on, and the bitter blast drives him from the mountains. Subdued by hunger, he wanders to the solitary shielings of the shepherds and will sometimes follow them through the snow, with irresolute steps, as they are carrying provender to the sheep.

He falls, perhaps, into moss-pits and mountain tarns whilst in quest of decayed water plants, where he perishes prematurely from utter inability to extricate himself. Many, again, who escape starvation, feed too greedily on coarse herbage at the first approach of open weather, which produces a murrain amongst them, not unlike the rot in sheep, of which they frequently die.

Thus, natural causes, inseparable from the condition of deer in a northern climate, and on a churlish soil unsheltered by woods, conspire to reduce these animals to so feeble a state that the short summer which follows is wholly unsufficient to bring them to the size they are capable of attaining under better management.

The strongest and most adaptable survive, even without special feeding. Highland friends who think that hand-feeding is unwise claim that a forest owner should either improve the quality of the natural feed in the area or cull the deer to a level at which there is sufficient natural food for them. A substantial surplus of deer has to be culled to keep the population at a level acceptable to modern ideas of land-use. Each year man, taking the role of principal predator, thins Scottish herds by rifle shot, disposing of over thirty thousand stags and hinds.

Among the departing stags seen near the Devil's Elbow was a *switch*, an animal whose Gaelic name is *caberslach*. The antlers sport only the lower (brow) tines and are thus more deadly in rutting combat than antlers carried by orthodox beasts. The *switch*, a potentially dangerous type, is quickly eliminated.

I pitied the red deer stags trudging across their wintry moor until I saw five roe deer moving much higher up the hill, at over 1,500 feet. And I had thought of the roe as a softish animal adorning the valley woodland.

Distance, and the blinding whiteness of the snow across which they walked, rendered them as dark silhouettes, yet they were recognisably roe, clad in thick, grey-tipped winter coats. These were assumed in autumn, at which time the bucks had cast their antlers. Charles St John recorded that from May to October roe "are covered with bright red brown hair, and but little of it. In winter their coat is a fine dark mouse-colour, very long and close, but the hair is brittle and breaks easily in the hand like dried grass. . . ."

I left the deer in their high and treeless habitat, where they bed in rank heather, yet of all the sights I saw that day I remember them most clearly—five diminutive roe picking their way across a high snowfield, and stopping from time to time to eat who knows what?

Having heard much about the Devil's Elbow, all accounts stressing the dangers of the place, I was chastened at finding that the Elbow no longer exists. Gone is the famous switchback, with its black and white railings. The Devil was sent packing by the road authorities, though a Devil's Staircase may be found near Glencoe and, much nearer, there is a Devil's Kitchen near the head of Glen Callater, the latter a crag. Does the Devil brew up all the bad weather here?

Mist draped the head of Cairnwell hill, but chairs on the lift were moving in the murk, travelling slowly, mysteriously vanishing into a sullen, damp greyness. Near the late-lamented Devil's Elbow was a group of buildings that look more Swiss than Highland in character and represent a late stage in a sport-

ing revolution beginning in the 1930s, when efforts were made
to establish a ski centre. Braemar was the first choice. The war
intervened.

Scottish ski enterprises date mainly from the 1950s, when
there was activity at the head of Glen Clunie. Many still
remember the wartime skiers, troops being trained as specialists
in mountain warfare. Ski-ing in Scotland was in the nature of a
refresher course for the Norwegians and Poles who were drafted
temporarily to the Highlands. Incidentally, Glen Shee was the
third of the chairlift centres. Here, sipping coffee, I watched a
coin being slipped into a juke box and prepared to flee. The item
selected, "Amazing Grace", filled the cafe with reverberating
bagpipe music, so I stayed.

Up here the world was white and it was hard to recall the
sunny Perthshire fields. Presumably they were still sunny, glowing with the light red of ploughed ground and the green of the
road verges. Snow had fallen before Christmas, but the main
blizzards swept the area in January. It was hoped that there
would be enough snow until after Easter (and, indeed, this was
the case, as I saw when I returned to Cairnwell in May).

A young man drove by on a snow-scooter. Cars were continually arriving to claim spaces in the capacious parking
ground. Ten yards from where my vehicle came to rest a group
of birds pecked at food thrown out by early visitors, who were
now recreating up in the mist. Another bird perched at the edge
of a snowdrift, a foot away from a litter basket and I gazed at
a snow bunting.

Thousands of snow buntings descend on Britain in autumn,
and their temporary quarters are in geographical extremes—
either high hills or sea coast. The buntings depart north for
their nesting grounds about March, though a few stay behind
and breed in remote Cairngorm scree-beds. Naturalists who
watch snow buntings so readily at Glen Shee—or, indeed, around
the car park at the approach to the Cairn Gorm chairlift, in
Speyside—break down and whimper on walking themselves to
a standstill looking for a nest in some of Britain's most demand-

Descent from the Devil's Elbow towards the Spital of Glen Shee

Church at the Spital of Glen Shee

Looking back towards the Spital of Glen Shee from the higher reaches of the Cairnwell pass

One of the chairs at the Glen Shee lift, looking towards Glen Clunie

ing countryside. The nesting birds have usually been eyeing them in a not unfriendly fashion throughout the scorching day!

I wondered, seeing snow buntings shuffling over an inch or two of frozen snow at two thousand feet by the Cairnwell, how many of them had real reason to fear man, a stranger to them until the migratory journey began. The birds were not exactly tame nor confiding. They were living their lives close to man because he had invaded their wintering grounds and showed no belligerency towards them. And meanwhile they had discovered that man was inclined to leave a trail of edibles behind him— even, on occasion, to toss some food in their direction!

Living in wintry surroundings the year through, the buntings were not daunted by the conditions that morning. They shuffled along, pecked at food or let the stiff wind carry them to other rewarding feeding areas. They called out, a rapid sequence of notes, each note having the clarity of a well-cast bell.

When snow buntings arrive in Britain there can be flocks of considerable size. A friend watched a group of two hundred birds. An especially large flock seen on the northern Pennines consisted of 350–400 birds, among which were a few Lapland buntings. Our snow buntings come mainly from Iceland and northern Scandinavia, and their plumage is drabber than that worn during the hectic far-northern spring.

The car park attendant by the Cairnwell Pass had seen a flock of up to twenty birds that winter. He took the birds into account when forecasting weather trends. "Snow buntings seem to turn up just before a snowfall. If there are no buntings, the snow which has fallen will largely go. Naturally I want to see snow buntings!"

This general comment would not satisfy a scientist, but it seemed to work out in practice. The man had been to the Lowlands to celebrate Hogmanay with friends. He arrived back at the chairlift the following day. Buntings were present on the car park and "snow fell soon afterwards".

Naturalists who have listed the food preferences of snow buntings, both here and in their northern nesting grounds, should add to the list details of the special fare the birds receive at Glen Shee. They like bread, cheese and even cream crackers. John Armitage and others, conducting detailed research into the food being taken by snow buntings on the southern Pennines, found a preference for *mollinia*, which the birds visited to feed on the clusters of gall-midge larvae infecting the haulms; they also took *mollinia* seeds. A good friend, Bill Robson, working the Westmorland Pennines, records that purple moor grass (locally common) and heath rush are also attractive to snow buntings.

At Glen Shee, the snow buntings shuffle about the car park until the traffic begins to build up, and then they move off, presumably to feed on the hillside. I saw a group leave the car park and alight near a pylon standing fifty yards from the road. There the birds stayed for a while.

There was a Pleistocene chill about the first part of the descent from the chairlift to Braemar. I moved through deep-blue shadows and between walls of snow which marked precisely the extent of the road. The roadmen were neat as well as efficient! When the road burst from shadow it began to meander between expanses of heather that glowed warmly in sunlight. The stump of a pole had been rubbed, presumably by deer.

There was a satin finish to the road, which was gradually being straightened as roadmen—fresh from their triumph at the Devil's Elbow—nibbled at the bends. Though historically a military way, the route was not quite as the army left it. The soldiers' good idea and hard work was developed far. Prince Albert and Colonel Farquharson had dipped into their purses to finance improvements in 1864.

In my progress towards Braemar I had to concentrate mainly on the road, but I also let my eyes wander to the line where a hill range to my right met the sky. I was looking for deer. Suddenly, the skyline was broken by the forms of half a dozen stags, in silhouette. The outlines might have been black paper stuck against the blue.

Over sixty stags inhabited the hillside, and all their eyes were directed towards the car as it drew to a halt. Stags lying between tufts of heather stopped their ponderous chewing of the cud as they contemplated my actions. They looked very comfortable with the sunlight fully upon them and the hill behind taking the raw edge from the wind. A stag maybe three hundred yards away relaxed; it languidly and ecstatically rubbed its head against a boulder. Other deer began to graze again. Cud-chewing was resumed by the recumbent beasts. The jaws worked rhythmically, with a sideways action, reducing their coarse grazings to a mush acceptable to their delicate digestive systems. I was fortunate to see the deer so composed and so near the road in daylight. If there had been wild weather, they would have tucked themselves out of sight in the corries.

As winter develops, red deer do not throng the low ground as a matter of course, for in mild conditions they are inclined to stay up high. In any case, stags are not as slavishly attached to particular areas as are the hinds. The low and sheltered ground is sought as the weather deteriorates—and in the eastern Highlands this usually means after Christmas. The deer may remain on low ground until May, returning to the heights when flies start biting and human visitors spread noisily across the glens.

I stayed in Glen Clunie until about an hour before dark, The sixty stags moved down the slopes and across the flat towards the road. Then the nearest beasts stood hesitantly one hundred yards from the car, with the rearguard of the herd still up the hill. In dull light the stags looked lighter in tone than the heather, much darker than the patches of coarse grasses lying between the heather tufts, and jet black when viewed against the banks of snow, through which—to my surprise—they did not hesitate to walk even when they could easily have moved round them.

Ignoring the direct approach to Braemar, I took the older route, crossing Fraser's Bridge over the Clunie—which is a fusion of several burns rippling from the Grampian snowfields—and seeing to the west a rounded hill, Morrone (2,819 feet), from which I once picked up some cast antlers. The name of the hill is derived from *mor bheinn*, meaning 'big hill'. Visitors climb it for staggeringly good views of the upper Dee.

The long, matted head of Morrone lies only 1,700 feet above the level of Braemar, and again I concentrated on the skyline, which soon was broken by a stag. Knowing where it stood helped me to locate a group of twenty two stags, some of which were grazing and others in placid recline. What do red deer think about during their long periods of rumination? A further twelve stags grazed an area where there was some 'black ground', and one of them fed on a circlet of heather exposed at the centre of a snowdrift, across which the deer's tracks were plain to see.

The Braemar district appeared to be living under siege conditions. There were deer fences on either side of the road, forming a curious aisle of netting and leading me to speculate what would happen if an excited stag found itself between the two lines of fencing with, perhaps, a motor cycle roaring in at speed.

In Braemar itself most of the householders had raised tall fences around their gardens. The lady who provided me with overnight accommodation said that her fence had withered away and, demoralised, she had not replaced it. The garden was now a prairie following some disheartening experiences of trying to grow delicacies like brussels sprouts, for which—not unnaturally—the red deer craved.

The raiding deer are not often seen. They arrive after dark and have taken themselves off to the hills well before the sun shows its face next morning. The lady with grassland for a garden said the deer do not care for daffodils but "they eat hyacinths, leaves and all. If deer get into a garden and develop a taste for something like sprouts they'll come back night after night until everything has been cleared." Then she added that "venison is nice—it's like beef!"

Everyone at Braemar has a tale about wintering deer—of stags suddenly revealed in the glare of car headlights; of animals clattering away into the darkness after being disturbed by pedestrians. Walking through the village at night, I stared hard and listened long, without detecting deer, though at dusk when I was motoring a few hundred yards from the western edge of the village I braked suddenly as two stags appeared on the road ahead. The deer were moving to the grazings by the river. My appearance speeded them up.

Next morning some fresh deer droppings lay on the garden path no more than ten yards from the room in which I slept!

4

A SLEEPING STAG

A few days before I crossed the Mounth I walked up to a red stag and stroked it. The animal slept peacefully on a couch of heather. Protruding from its haunches was a syringe that had been fired from a rifle. At the moment of impact a small plastic cap had been knocked away and into the deer went an amber-coloured liquid. The stag was anaesthetised, and while it lay unconscious a bright red tag was fixed to the lobe of an ear so that its future movements could be plotted.

The 'day of the darting' was typical for the Highlands. First there was a blaze of sunlight, and my eyes were seared. Strong directional light brought a sparkle to the lochs and the dun-coloured landscape appeared to smoulder. A steady deterioration of the weather began in the early afternoon when a curtain of cloud was slowly drawn across the face of the sun and the air became numbingly cold. Grey conditions continued. There were a few flakes of snow—well-spaced flakes that invited me to count them.

The stags chosen for the demonstration of tranquillisation and tagging were assembled at the edge of a deer forest in which there was a tradition of winter feeding. I asked a stalker how far it was from the lodge (where we stood) to the first of the deer, and he replied, "A wee while." This was about a mile!

As I chuckled at his vagueness, he told me a story from his

youth—of how a stalker described a certain place as lying "a mile and a bit" away. The visitor who needed this information returned in due course and said he had enjoyed the mile "but the 'bit' nearly killed me"!

Our journey to the red deer feeding ground began at a low level—for the Highlands, that is. The lodge stood near a loch that had a fringe of birches. The loch gleamed in the diffused light with the hard intensity of a mirror and beyond it lay some old 'black woods', as areas of pine are known. Further back, the highest hills were tormented by squalls of sleet or snow. The stalker said there were golden eagles, ptarmigan and white hares on those hills. Hares were particularly common. He had seen the slopes "black with white hares".

Two buzzards circled at a moderate height above the lodge, and their occasional mewing reached us clearly, for there was little wind. Another large brown bird cleared the tops of some pines maybe half a mile away and it stayed in view for several minutes. The stalker said, matter-of-factly, without trace of emotion, "An eagle."

The mewing of buzzards had a restful, Sunday afternoonish sound that accentuated rather than destroyed a feeling of peace with the world. Then a tractor passed with a roar; it was drawing a trailer full of brewers' chaff, which is nutritious to cattle.

The stags waiting for us on the moor knew the stalker, whom they saw twice a day in winter. They recognised the general tone of his clothes, but more particularly the manner of his walk and the resonance of the voice that called them loudly to the food he provided.

Two Highland ponies, or garrons, recognised the stalker, who used them to bring dead stags from the hills during the season. Garrons, which wear special saddles, are becoming redundant on the hill now that several types of powerful four-wheel-drive vehicles can easily negotiate burns and rough ground. "These machines don't think for themselves," said the stalker, in defence of garrons.

One of the garrons—the "big brown fellow"—was about

twenty years old and ready for a pension. The other, dun-
coloured, was entering the prime of its life at five years. Both
stood at about 14 hands high. The stalker could foretell a time
when there would be no garrons on the deer forest. This type
of pony was being used for pony-trekking, but "there's been a
mixing-up of blood. Garrons are being cross-bred with such
types as hunters. It's very sad."

Seeing the garrons, and talking about these docile animals,
opened up a vein of reminiscence. The stalker told me he began
work on the hill as a pony boy. "You can't get boys to work the
ponies now. Lads have no interest in anything that hasn't got a
gear and clutch."

The garrons he managed were always pure-bred, with a dark
stripe along the spine. "That is a pretty good sign that you've
got the right type of animal." A garron has a broad back but is
not necessarily heavy. "It develops its own pace on the hill.
Can't go too fast with a dead stag on its back. The deer's body
tends to swing. A garron has a steady pace—it's steady in everything, even living. I've known garrons to be working at twenty-
five years old. One was still useful at twenty eight."

We left the enclosed ground for the deer forest. I had a vista
of pearl-white hills. Over five hundred stags roamed this estate,
plus about four hundred and twenty hinds, which frequented
separate areas. The largest stag, a fifteen-pointer, had been
tagged two years before.

Feeding stags, part of the winter routine for several years, led
to a great improvement in the quality of the beasts, particularly
in the size of their heads. Good heads were no longer shot, so
the landowner was thinking of the future.

With the stalker I stood on the "vacant wine-red moor", a
little apart from the company that had assembled to watch the
darting. The stalker was, like the most elderly garron I had seen,
a little past his best. He was, indeed—and not to make too fine
a point—an elderly man, but lean-faced, with a fresh com-
plexion, and pale-blue eyes that missed nothing. The man's
body, long and lish, was swaddled in tweed. By his manner and

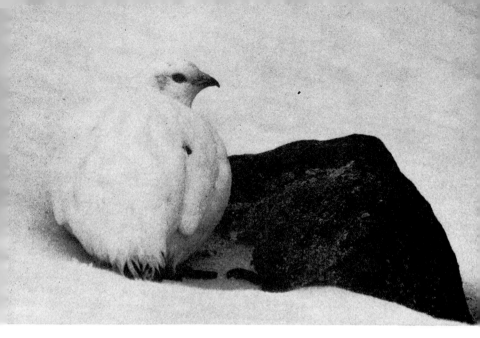

Ptarmigan in winter plumage

Captive wild cat

Captive red grouse

speech he gave the impression of being as much at home on the hill as were the deer themselves. He would remember the grandparents of the present stock!

As a stalker, he was one of a class of Highlander that represents the ultimate refinement of a long deer-hunting tradition. Once there was mass murder of Highland fauna, with relentless hunting by the clans in vast drives called *tainchels*. The deer—and whatever else was caught up in the drive—were forced into confined areas, even into stone enclosures, and butchery took place with bows and blunderbusses, the luckless animals providing a spectacle of sorts but being also regarded as so much protein on the hoof. In these days of supermarkets and deep freezes we cannot imagine how deeply our ancestors craved for protein.

Stalking is a modern phenomenon. It flowered with the development of sporting guns. The hunters were no longer plain hungry or lusting for a spectacle worthy of a Hollywood epic, but seeking to outwit a good stag—to fell it with a single shot after a hard slog. The stalker, a local man, would take a sportsman surreptitiously to within a few score yards of the right animal.

The stalker told me of his exacting apprenticeship to the hill. As a young man he was appointed a ghillie, which is apparently Gaelic for a hired junior. Then he became a ponyman, leading a garron to the stalking ground and eventually returning with two hundredweights of dead stag. It sounds simple, but a good ponyman was also building up in his mind an intimate picture of the hills, weather lore and the ways of birds and beasts. He needed to know *all* about hill life, for red deer do not exist in a vacuum.

Later, as a walking ghillie, he carried the rifle of the sportsman and also *gralloched* the animal that was slain. All the time he planned for his future life as a stalker, a folk hero in the Highlands. When this job came to him he outwitted stags, kept his temper in the presence of any dim-witted sportsmen and rejoiced with those who shot a stag cleanly. And when the

D

visitors had gone home—when, indeed, the Highlands were at their stormy worst—the stalker culled the surplus hinds, alone and temporarily forgotten.

This elderly man's life had been spent in a relatively quiet world, but now the hills were echoing to the roar of engines—of Land-Rover, Haflinger and Sno Track. No-one, he pointed out emphatically, had yet devised a mechanical stalker!

There were stags in view long before our vehicle had drawn up near the feeding area. Red deer were silhouetted on the nearest horizon, and elsewhere they stood as indeterminate shapes, for the day was overcast and gloomy. The deer converging on the feeding ground detected in the air a subtle aroma compounded of maize, hay, deer cob and potato. They also recognised the routine.

Stags moving below the horizon had a tonal harmony with the moor. Their coarse, dark-brown winter hair blended visually with coarse, dark-brown heather. The deer were tinged with grey, and grey and white were also represented on the moor as lingering snow-drifts. The stags moved with the regal gait of their kind, taking long and even strides, holding up their heads, displaying widespread antlers.

Now there were stags milling near the parked vehicles. The animals were uneasy, moving briskly as though centuries of association with man had taught them not to stand still. The denseness of the winter coat, and the prominent manes added to their size. A stag turned and briefly revealed a heart-shaped speculum. Against the cream of the rump lay the brown dorsal surface of the tail.

Deer under natural conditions would feed mainly at dawn and dusk; they would lie up in some secure area during the brightest part of the day, with their backs to the wind, chewing the cud, cat-napping with ears half-cocked. Does a deer ever sleep as we know sleep, putting mind and body into neutral for hours on end? I have the impression that they get through life by briefly dozing.

These deer were lucky to receive regular rations. The wild

stock, living entirely off the ground, had to climb up to the places where the wind had blown off the snow and exposed moss and lichen, or they would scrape away snow crystals with their forefeet to expose the heather. Many could find welcome grazing ground in the corries.

The member of our party who was to demonstrate the darting of deer assembled his modified .22 rifle. Gas would be used as the propellant for the syringe, which would not travel with a flat trajectory, curving instead like the course taken by a dart to a board. The distance had to be assessed exactly so that the dart would hit the deer in a good place (ideally, the haunch) at the end of the curve. An effective distance is from fifty to sixty yards, yet the gun can operate from one hundred to two hundred yards and, with adaptation, might also be used at close range—even three feet.

There was a "thwack" as the gun spoke. It was not the normal, reverberating crack of the sporting rifle. Momentarily the assembled deer were startled, pricking up their ears, lifting their heads to taste the air. The deer resumed their milling around tousled heaps of best clover hay.

The stag that received the dart was irritated rather than annoyed. Did it associate the slight pain with some devilish biting insect? The dart could be seen sticking from a haunch. For a time the stag could not be readily distinguished from the rest of the herd, and then its movements became slurred and it assumed a dreamy manner that contrasted with the alertness of the beasts around it. The nearest stags were fascinated by its untypical, blundering behaviour.

Sitting down on its haunches, the stag was undignified, like a dog begging for food. The head lolled, first to one side, then to the other. Slowly and rather wearily the animal went over on its side, yet it made several attempts to raise its head before the effect of the anaesthetic was total. Even then some of the nerves twitched.

Walking over to the deer I stroked its head for the novelty of touching a wild animal. It was a tough old stag, maybe fifteen years old, which is a good life span for a Highlander. A beast is long past its best at the age of twelve.

For the first time since it was born, and rose tremblingly to its feet to seek out the teat of its parent hind and to take in the first long draughts of milk that is six times more nourishing than the cow's milk we drink, the stag was insensitive to its environment. The sights, sounds, even the tang of the hill meant nothing.

The age of the stag was surprising. The stern conditions on the hill, and long winters leading to weeks of deprivation, are not conducive to longevity. It is estimated that less than 10 per cent of the red deer population in the Highlands is over eight years old. Round about half the calves that are born perish before their first year is completed. Nature is therefore particularly hard on the very young and the very old.

The marksman opened the stag's mouth and clicked his tongue in sympathy with the animal. There were cracked or broken teeth. He decided to improve the stag's ability to graze by removing some of the troublesome molars. This was achieved by a deft handling of pliers, and then the red tag was pressed on to the ear of the animal.

When I first became aware of the stag as an individual, shortly after it had been hit by the dart, I thought that the large area where the hair was pressed flat was associated with the impact of the dart. It was now revealed as a large, dark, glistening abscess. The marksman, a qualified veterinary surgeon, neatly lanced the abscess, and from it gushed a torrent of khaki liquid that had a strong and unpleasant smell. When the wound had drained he injected penicillin and then the antidote to the drug originally administered. We stood back and watched the stag return to consciousness.

Recovery was slow. The deer remained motionless on the heather, its tongue protruding from between dry lips. At an appropriate time, as the deer struggled to rise, the marksman helped the stag into a sitting position and then it was persuaded to rise to its legs, as yet weak and disorientated. The stag sat down on its haunches. At that moment there was something pathetically comical about this monarch of the glen!

The animal was again helped on to its feet. It stood, wobbling, but there began a slow, hesitant progress away from the area. The stag would soon recover—and doubtless feel rather more comfortable than it had following the lancing of the abscess. I suggested to the marksman that he had given the stag the equivalent of a 10,000 mile service for a car. He thought it was an appropriate comparison.

A second stag we darted was a youngish animal, about three years old. The dart caught it low on a hind leg but the drug worked quickly and eventually the recovery was more rapid than in the case of the first stag. Struggling gamely to its feet, the youngster made off between lines of spectators and with its head held low.

We returned to the lodge. The buzzards were still riding the upper air currents. It was pleasant to hear their cat-like mewing, for I could not recall a single natural sound heard during my stay at the edge of the gloomy deer forest.

5

BIRD OF THE HEATHER

Two dark blotches lay on the glaring snowfield at rather more than two thousand feet above sea-level, close to the Cairnwell Pass. They were red grouse—more precisely cock grouse, tough moorland characters living out their adulthood only a mile or so from the places where they were hatched. The red grouse, denizen of the treeless moor, where heather and blaeberry sprout from peat that obtrudes like slabs of chocolate cake, is one of Scotland's stay-at-homes.

Two Highland names for the red grouse are 'gor-cock' and 'muirfowl'. To me the cock grouse will always be a 'moorcock', and seeing the two birds close at hand made me feel thoroughly at home. Most of my life has been spent within half a dozen miles of moorland—and grouse.

One of the grouse I now surveyed flew off, its stubby wings whirring as it built up power that would carry its podgy form to speeds at which it could intersperse flying with gliding. The grouse banked, then gained a little height to suit the changing contours of the hill. Whizzing low over the road, maybe seventy yards away from me, the grouse pitched down in some heather that had managed to keep its head above the drifts.

The other bird preferred a laboured retreat. It surged forward, breasting the snow, working its legs hard, and leaving deep impressions of feet and body on an otherwise pristine landscape.

When it was impelled to fly it burst from the ground explosively. The flight—like that of the other grouse—closely matched the contours.

Another cock, higher up the hill, began to cackle. Its voice, with a disturbingly human quality, was that traditionally rendered, "go back, go back, go back". Walkers traditionally ignore it. I recalled the time I returned the shout from a range of three feet. A gamekeeper trod on a hen grouse while walking his moors. He had killed the bird but found that most of the eggs beneath it were whole. The eggs were transported to his home croft and hatched out under broody bantams. Here, months later, he invited me to see his grouse. Among them was a splended cock which advanced across its pen and shouted at me from a range of a few feet. If there had been no wire netting between us I am sure it would have flown at me. The bird crowed, "go back", and those were the words I used in the hope of persuading it to move further back so that I could photograph it. The grouse was not amused when I gave the words something like the intonation it employed!

That gamekeeper had no success in rearing the grouse, for they were unsuitable for sporting purposes. He reared them, it is true, having had the wit to transport from his moor some turves festooned with heather and bilberry, but the birds had lost the wild spirit for which he craved. He told me, rather sadly, that if he had released them they would have perched at the end of the gun barrels on the Glorious Twelfth.

A Speyside grouse was unlike the majority of the wild stock, being so confiding with man it came to hand. As the date for grouse shooting approached this bird was lured into a pen and kept there until the danger of its being shot was over. These are exceptional cases. The only prison tolerated by the red grouse is an ecological one. Subsisting mainly on heather, the grouse is virtually a prisoner on the moors.

I was in the Highlands during a comparatively mild winter— one of several in succession—and the grouse were not under stress. Snow cover was not continuous, and the snow itself was powdery, slipping through the fingers like fine sand. It could thus be easily shifted by grouse seeking food.

The worst combination of weather, said a Highland keeper, is when deep snow becomes crusted over with ice. The grouse find it difficult to break through the crust. "This happened in the winter of 1962–3. The grouse simply disappeared from some areas. Where they went to, no-one seems to know."

During that winter I saw a small pack of grouse in a village street. Other packs were reported to have settled on the main road. To survive, grouse must be able to reach heather and also supplies of the quartz grit that assists with the breakdown of the tough food.

Snow by itself is not much of a problem. A grouse treads it underfoot as it falls. Lloyd (he who secured Swedish capercaillie, helping to reintroduce this largest of the grouse family to Britain) studied willow grouse in Scandinavia and was possibly the first to report that in winter they sometimes make burrows in the snow in which they shelter from climatic excesses.

Willow grouse and red grouse are the same species. Our red is the local variant. At the approach of winter the willow grouse —like the ptarmigan—assumes a white plumage, but the red grouse lives in a region where there are few severe winters. Pure white plumage would clearly be a disadvantage on the dark moors.

When winter comes, the red grouse has moulted into a drabber plumage than the reddish-brown of summer. It remains a colourful bird when viewed against coarse grass and loses itself in the heather, with which it so wonderfully tones. The wintering grouse has white leg feathers, like avian spats.

Red grouse pack in severe weather. They jag (roost) in loose groups. When there are mild spells the cock grouse shows some territorial inclinations. A tract of rough ground that to you or me is worthless becomes, to the moorcock, the focal point of its existence, to be fiercely defended. Birds have been known to pair up as early as January, though eggs are laid in late April. This time can be more severe weatherwise than the earlier date.

The first nesters withstand blizzards and, with frosty nights even in May, many a hen grouse continues to sit its egg clutch as snow drifts around the nest.

Take away the heather, and the red grouse perishes. This is happening indirectly as conifer plantations are established on moorland. *Calluna vulgaris*, the common ling, is bread if not butter to the grouse. Its twin—the willow grouse—subsists in its bleak northlands partly on the buds of trees.

The scientists of the Nature Conservancy's unit concerned with grouse and moorland have studied the bird as never before, but I kept some of the findings of the grouse disease committee, which years ago examined the crops of about 1,500 red grouse as part of its inquiries. The dependence on *Calluna* was clearly shown. Heather shoots formed 60 per cent of the diet of the bird in December, 64 per cent in January, 75 per cent in February and 97 per cent in March. Early on, *Calluna* seedheads were eaten. During the last two months the grouse's food included the stalks and buds of blaeberry.

Nature Conservancy conclusions indicate that it is the territorial behaviour shown in autumn that determines the size of the grouse's breeding stock in the following year. The most thrustful cocks obtain territories and, eventually, the hens to go with them (one hen per cock is the general rule). These birds endure and breed. The quite large population of less successful birds suffers a fearful mortality during the winter or, through a variety of causes, in the following spring.

In my journey I noticed that the territorial impulses of grouse were already strong. Displaying cock birds rose, breasted the cold wind, almost stopped in mid-air, then descended, wings beating slowly, in a flight somewhat reminiscent of the springtime shuttlecock flight of meadow pipits. Meanwhile, the grouse called. The sounds seemed unduly passionate in an area patched with snow.

Grouse are, in their turn, food for other creatures. Battered corpses are seen near the earths of foxes and in the eyries of golden eagles. Hooded crows filch the eggs. Many creatures find the young grouse palatable. Each August, the grouse-shooters are out and about, settling in the butts while beaters rouse the grouse and send them winging towards destruction. Falconers in Glencoe used peregrines in the hunting of grouse. The grouse were flushed from cover by pointers, and the falcons stooped on the disturbed birds. Falconry is less efficient than driving to the butts—if the size of the kill is what really matters—but the supporters consider it to be more exciting to observe.

Grouse thrive nowhere better in Scotland than on the eastern moors. A grouse moor may be adjacent to a deer forest (you would be hard put to it, if asked to distinguish between the two, to identify them by simply looking). On the grouse moor the bird is all, heather is burnt off in rotation to encourage the development of fresh shoots and predators are shot. Grouse that live in a deer forest have a nuisance value to those whose joy is in stalking deer. The grouse's condition or fate are not taken seriously into account, and stalkers curse under their breath when they disturb a covey of birds which then goes off, whirring and shouting, alerting the deer.

Man tries to get the most out of a grouse moor. Keepers worry and fret their way through the ever-changing year. They are despondent when the spring is cold and wet and there is a high mortality of chicks. They conduct relentless war against crows and foxes. Yet, says the Nature Conservancy, following investigation of the ecology of moorland, in the end it is the grouse that calls the tune. This species can regulate its population to suit the carrying capacity of the moor.

Certainly if a moor is stocked far beyond its natural holding capacity many problems must be faced, not least the threat of disease. Keepers have told me that the autumnal cull, carried out by sportsmen, should be heavy so that comparatively few birds remain. But if, for some reason, a grouse moor is under-populated the owner cannot scurry off to a hatchery for grouse chicks he can rear. The moorcock does not like being molly-coddled.

Hearing the becking of a grouse up by the Cairnwell pass I

spun round and localized it. Only the neck and wattled head were visible, and then only through powerful binoculars. I respect the grouse. The bird in sight might have hatched out during a blizzard from an egg that was stung by frost before the completion of the clutch, when the hen bird was ready to incubate. During its comparatively short life the grouse had lived in a treeless area, panted in the summer heat and been washed by seventy or eighty inches of rain each year. Winter gales had pelted it with hail, sleet or snow. This bird had survived even the rain of lead pellets from the butts the previous autumn.

Now, a fine cock in its territory, it called while strutting between the tufts of ling. I tried to imitate its call. The grouse looked interested but did not come forward as I hoped. Richard Kearton, pioneer wildlife photographer, took a first step on the road to fame when attending the head of a London publishing firm who was visiting the grouse moors and showed disappointment at the misty conditions that rendered sport impossible. The lad imitated the mewing call of a hen bird. It worked. Several cocks came forward to investigate.

The visitor had his sport—and he offered Kearton a job!

6

BRAEMAR AND BEYOND

At Braemar I was virtually ringed by high hills. Their predominance did not escape the attention of an early visitor who left a record of his experiences. About the year 1618 the Dee valley was entered by John Taylor. He arrived "with extreme travell, ascending and descending, mounting and alighting".

Taylor found himself in "a large country, all composed of such mountains that Shooter's hill, Gad's hill, Highgate hill, Hampstead hill, Birdliphill or Malvernes hill are but mole-hills in comparison, or like a hive, or a gizard under a capon's wing, in respect of the altitude of their tops or perpendicularitie of their bottoms".

I scanned the hills slowly and appreciatively—and then walked stiff-necked into a cafe whose tables were adorned by tartan cloths. Later, being at Braemar, I dutifully 'did' some of the local sights. There was the hallowed ground used for the Games, and the house in which Robert Louis Stevenson spent seven weeks during August and September 1881. He wrote to please a young relative and also possibly to help him forget the prevailing weather, which was wet. And the masterpiece—for such it became—was *Treasure Island*. A man of Stevenson's stature could write vividly about the sea and ships and a remote island while staying in a cleft between misty hills many miles from the coast!

Braemar, its character derived from its situation and royal

benevolence, is not conspicuously old. Most of it, indeed, is no older than 1871, when there was the start of a rebuilding boom. Hanging on the landing wall of my guest house was a photograph of a building that would be one of the last of the old type —a hovel with low rough walls and a thatched roof. This was the sort of domestic architecture seen by Queen Victoria during her first Deeside jaunts.

Pennant, about a century earlier, noted that "the houses of the common people in these parts are shocking to humanity, formed of loose stones and covered with clods, which they call *divots*". The thatching was formed with a base of 'heath-brown' or fir branches. From a distance a thatched building of Pennant's day looked like a black mole-hill.

Having been critical of the architecture, Pennant considered the way of life of the people. "The inhabitants lived very poorly on oatmeal, barley-cakes and potatoes; their drink whisky, sweetened with honey." If anyone can afford to drink whisky today they may still have their honey. Bee-keeping is a local obsession judging by the number of hives. Bees range up to two miles from their quarters seeking nectar, and the highpoint of the Braemar year must come in autumn, when the ling is flowering, yielding—via the bees—the appetising heather honey, which is so viscid it cannot be taken from the combs in the normal way.

Whisky was distilled in "sma' stills" set in the remoter glens. The spirit was then smuggled by men who remained fairly inconspicuous by using a web of minor routes, though among the customers were soldiers stationed at Braemar Castle, which was restored as a barracks following the Jacobite troubles. Men were billeted here until 1831.

In commending Deeside to the world through her example and writings, Queen Victoria made Braemar one of the best-known villages in Scotland. The effect of publicity on a national scale has been demonstrated again at Callander, where some filming took place for the long-running television series, *Dr Finlay's Casebook*. The Queen wrote so enthusiastically

about her life in the Highlands that those with money and time
on their hands emulated her and travelled over the Mounth or
up the valley from Aberdeen. They found (as I have already
indicated) a rather miserable little village of some good homes
but many thatched hovels.

The Water of Clunie divides Braemar into two. Once the
demarcation based on the river was accentuated by rivalries
between local estates, those of Mar and Invercauld. The Mar
influence was strong in Castleton, a community that developed
around Kindrochit Castle (Kindrochit means 'head of the
bridge'). The castle, established towards the end of the four-
teenth-century, had become ruined by the seventeenth century.
Now it is a heap of stones. The people in Auchindryne ('thorny
land') of Invercauld doffed their hats to the Farquharsons.

If stones could speak, those of Kindrochit would tell of
Malcolm III, whose hunting seat it was. Malcolm, incidentally,
overthrew the better-known Macbeth. Victorian landowners
were just as zealous in preserving deer stocks for sport, but they
—unlike Malcolm—were not prepared to let nature take her
course. Do any pure Highland red deer remain?

The Earl of Fife introduced wapiti, presumably to develop
better, larger animals without thought of the type best suited to
the locality—and that was the one already there! I was told
that wapiti will stand for a red stag, but that no self-respecting
hind would allow itself to be covered by a wapiti stag. The
question of dilution of old Highland blood by foreign types was
too fine a point for me to argue, and there was little help from
the works of Victorian sportsmen I consulted. Indeed, there was
much muddled thinking revealed by Walter Winans, F.Z.S.,
who wrote *Deer Breeding for Fine Heads* in 1913. His observations were at least interesting.

Winans had heard a good deal of talk about the deterioration
of the Highland red deer heads by the introduction of park and
German stags into Scottish deer forests for the purpose of
improving the heads. He personally thought that the old Highland head died out long ago—before he began stalking in 1870.

What he regarded as the true Highland head was the type seen in the illustrations to Scrope's *Days of Deer Stalking* and in some of Landseer's pictures, "the main characteristic being the great amount of curl in the points of the horns, like the flourishes old masters of penmanship used to make in writing".

Winans had never seen a living stag with such horns, "but specimens of the type are preserved in old Scotch castles. . . . Seeing, then, that there is no living Highland head, it is useless to complain that the type is being spoilt, and the only thing to do is to try to breed the best possible heads of the Continental type. . . . It is curious that Scotch stags are at the present time the worst in Europe."

On the Continent the greatest care was taken to improve deer, "but in Scotland the general rule seems to be to kill every big stag that can be seen, without any reference to the future good of the herd. . . . What would be thought of the breeder of horses or cattle who killed every good animal he bred and only kept the trash? And yet this is just the way most Scotch forests are managed."

Perhaps the roaring of the Highland stags could help us to determine their pedigree. Winans noted that "the roar of the bull wapiti is quite different from that of the red deer stag, being much higher and going off into a high harmonic note. The wapiti-red deer cross begins with the red deer roar and ends in the wapiti whistle. . . ."

Scottish deer men today would need a week to argue out the points that Winans raised and expounded on so swiftly.

I left Braemar early one morning. Lichen-plated birches—*birks*, in the Highland parlance—stand in loose ranks to the left of the road, extending for most of the six miles westwards to the Linn of Dee. In England, the birch is generally accounted to be the 'weed of the woods'. It is reverenced in the Highlands, where it provides a decorative touch to the landscape without blotting out any views. The silver-and-black of its trunk has a festive air even on gloomy winter days, and when golden birch leaves shimmer in a light October breeze the massed trees make an impressive contribution to autumn's beauty. Yet the birch does not live for long—maybe sixty to eighty years, by which time it has been considerably rotted by fungi. The life-span of the average *birk* is about that of an average man.

The birches I saw standing slim and gay at the roadside near Braemar were descendants of ancient Scottish stock. Birch was the first true tree to break into the tundral barrens following the melting of Pleistocene ice. Today, these trees—and the ling and blaeberry that find adequate light while growing at their feet—give a wilderness flavour to the doorstep of Braemar. The wilderness began at the very edge of the road, for there was no curb, no pavement, no expanse of brilliant sown grass to detract from the tousled natural beauty.

A patch of white flashed between the *birks*. It was a rosette of feathers sported by an amorous blackcock—male of the black grouse species, now disporting itself only twelve feet from the road and a few hundred yards from the last house in the village.

Black grouse tend tò be traditionalists over the matter of displaying grounds; they cheerfully use old haunts even when the local topography has changed radically. When a forest road was laid across a *lek*, spring assembly ground of the blackcock, in another part of Scotland, the birds assembled on the road where, in previous years, they had displayed at first light, and the tradition was continued. Surely there was no *lek* among the birches near the road.

The blackcock turned. A strong light fell on its bulky form, and the dark plumage was seen to be sheened with bottle-green. Framing the white rosette were the black crescents of the tail which, in recline, takes on a lyre shape familiar to anyone who has seen a Highlander's bonnet. The scarlet combs on the bird's head were inflated and with good reason. Standing a few feet from the handsome male bird were five females—greyhens, so called, though the tone of their plumage has a brownish appearance, being finely barred with black.

The mildness of the winter could be deduced from the fact that I had heard of blackcocks assembling at some Scottish *leks*

One of the Deeside 'linns' with a relict area of Caledonian pine
forest beyond

(*top*) Braemar Castle (*bottom*) Above the Linn of Dee

as early as January. The display of the birds is normally seen at its best from the middle of March into April. My blackcock was a solo suitor with an outstanding array of female talent.

A greyhen took fright, and the excitement spread like a pond ripple to the others. Five necks stretched upwards, quizzically. A nervous bird became airborne, flicking itself aloft with quick, shallow wing beats and displaying white wing bars. The other greyhens followed, their wings beating vigorously until they were able to glide. When the momentum of the forward thrust was expended, another period of wing-beating began. No calls were uttered. There was just a rustle of feathers in the still air.

Finally the females were followed by the cock bird, whose white wing bars were even more clearly seen, the dark feathers around them providing the maximum contrast. The cock banked between the birches and was lost to sight. When flushing black grouse on an open hill, I have noticed a tendency for them to fly high, zooming aloft like missiles and sometimes circling to have another look at the cause of the disturbance. This characteristic can sometimes be exploited by sportsmen.

When the black grouse had gone I switched my attention to a roebuck—small, lightly-built, in grey winter coat, the antlers not yet fully developed and swathed in velvet. The deer bounded away rather casually over tussocky ground. Our friend Walter Winans, writing just before the 1914–18 war, which led to immense social changes, observed that in Scotland roe were considered of little account, "and are often bagged with the shotgun in covert-shooting, nothing being thought of the heads". I recall the interest shown in one of the annual exhibitions of Scottish heads organised by the Deer Society signifying that times have changed greatly since Winans was active.

He mentioned, incidentally, that a few Siberian roe had been turned out and they "might perhaps improve the heads of the native breed. . . ." The Victorians and Edwardians seemed to be embarrassed about the quality of the native stock and did all they could to change it.

The road to the Linn of Dee is a ledge cut from the hillside.

E

Birches give way to pines. One pine had been felled, exposing the orangy-red heartwood and its creamy surround. Slivers of gnarled grey bark lay at the circumference of the cut. Lichen was clinging to the branches that lay all around.

Old folk at Braemar had told me that before the 1939–45 war good timber stood virtually all the way from Braemar to Inverey, and there were large trees beyond here to the Linn of Dee, where the wild country begins. Canadian lumbermen toppled thousands of pines as their contribution to the war effort. The Canadians brought the flavour of the backwoods to Deeside with their lumber camps and extravagant behaviour. They built a wooden bridge across the Dee, a bridge that stood firm against the surge of the river for about twenty years.

Nature would ultimately have healed the old sores. Impatient man was giving nature a hand by setting down ranks of nursery-reared conifers. The trees stood primly, in neat rows, behind deerproof fencing.

A redundant stretch of the old road, left as a parking place for cars—and as a vantage point for visitors—would have been called 'Queen's View' if ancient guide book writers had their way. I prefer another title—'Peep o' Dee'. From it I peeped across Deeside to see Quoich at the entrance of its little pine-studded glen. The watercourse from that glen tumbled and then spread itself between broad fans of shingle.

The general tones of the valley were wintry, which does not mean that they were drab. Far from it. The colours extended from the rich browns of moorland and down through bottle-green pines to the pale yellows and verdant light greens of the flat fields. Here the grazing cattle would be joined by red deer at dusk.

The river looked shallow, but there was a hint of its manliness in the patches of white water that developed where it splashed against unseen obstructions, or boulders that were so smooth they looked like bald pates. The river's course lay close to the slope on the southern side of the valley, but soon the Dee would cut across to form an elegant loop near Braemar.

When the Cairngorms brew up storms of great violence, and rain falls in dense sheets, the Dee responds with equal severity. There have been times when a loch has formed in the valley. The most famous inundation was a 'muckle spate' in August. 1829. During a storm there was lightning "like broad bands of liquid fire". Every cloud emptied itself over the hills. The Dee grumbled and then overspilled. Soon it was running at about fifteen feet above normal.

The Dee was now well within its banks. It was left to the Corriemulzie burn, dashing to meet it near Inverey, to keep up the reputation for a spirited flow. Near the road the burn cascaded over rocks.

Having motored another half mile, I saw what might have been an English parkland. A white-painted Victorian bridge crossed the river to enter the grounds of what was a ducal residence, Mar Lodge. When there was a duke in residence this was the highest 'seat' in Britain, 1,250 feet above sea level.

The Scottish character was maintained by the rocks and conifers dominating the southern edge of the road, and here was the Gallows Tree o' Mar, appropriately in shade—a tall, barkless "drool dark pine" that wheezed in the wind and was supported by lengths of wire. Here was a sad memorial to the feudalism which enabled a noble to do as he pleased with the folk on his land. The Gallows Tree was not just a deterrent—it was used.

One of the Lamonts of Inverey, found to have "concealed strange beeves and muttons in his kill-logie", was strung up at the tree on the orders of the Farquharsons. The grieving mother, cursing the family, foretold that the tree would "flourish high and broad" when the Farquharsons died out. Just when the hanging occurred I do not know, but the direct line of the Farquharsons ended in 1806.

And, by uttering a curse that has been remembered, the mother ensured that her son would have his own special kind of immortality.

7

LINN O' DEE

The road breaks away from morning shadows at the junction of streams, from which geographical fact is named the clachan of Inverey. River Ey joins the Dee after tumbling down from the hills through a grassy glen. On the east bank stands Muckle Inverey, and Little Inverey is just across the water. Put the two together and you have scarcely enough buildings for a village.

The Sabbatic peacefulness of Inverey restrained me from knocking on any of the doors for further information. The silence must not be broken! If I had succeeded in attracting attention, would I have been received with a spate of Gaelic? Gibb and Hay found that the inhabitants clung to the Gaelic with great affection "although, at the same time, English is freely exchanged with visitors".

When they first heard Gaelic spoken they found it lacking in melody "but, though deficient of the smoothness of more polished tongues it is, notwithstanding, capable of expressing powerfully the strongest passion and the deepest sentiment".

The men of Inverey unselfconsciously wore the kilt; it was the fashionable dress. I wish I had knocked on one of the cottage doors out of curiosity. I might have heard a kilted man addressing me in the ancient tongue of Scotland!

Later I discovered that Gaelic was being spoken in this area as recently as 1880, so Edwin Landseer, the Victorian animal painter, may have had to cope with it. He liked Inverey, and from a local vantage point he made some of the studies that formed backgrounds to his large canvases. There is, for instance, a view of the Cairngorms behind the subject of his most famous painting, *The Monarch of the Glen*, which he completed in 1851.

Inverey, a small place, has history to spare. I heard a chilling story that the ghost of the Black Colonel haunted Muckle Inverey. He was John Farquharson, who lived through stormy days in the seventeenth century, using as a retreat a narrow cave eroded from the wall of a gorge by the dashing river Ey. The Colonel apparently spent much of his adult life fleeing from the redcoats, but he died peacefully in about 1698. His spirit refused to lie down, and it still prowls around.

The Colonel's tale, heard in Braemar, had already stimulated me to enter Glen Ey, in which one can feel very lonely within a mile or so of the main road. Perhaps one can still detect the sadness felt by several families who were cleared from the glen to make way for deer. There was no-one, not even the spirit of the Colonel, at the narrow cave-like formation known even today as his bed.

If someone had told me that I might see an eagle in this area I would have been in a fever of anticipation. Theoretically you can see an eagle in any part of Deeside. An eagle appeared from nowhere and after soaring for a while departed for who-knows-where? I did not investigate further, being content to know that eagles wing their way over the local deer forests. Mentioning the incident to the factor of a local estate, I was told that three eagles had circled high above his home the previous morning. Seeing them casually was all a matter of luck.

Eagles are possibly as common in Deeside as anywhere in Scotland. They do not flaunt themselves before the public gaze. A visitor must 'get his eye in' while looking for specks in the sky, forgetting the brilliantly-toned and regal bird he sees on a perch at a zoo. Views of eagles in the wild are seldom so good.

William MacGillivray, an expert on local natural history in

the middle of last century, yearned to see eagles. They were scarce in his day. "This species, which formerly existed in considerable numbers on Braemar, and bred in the precipices of the wilder glens, is now very seldom to be seen there," he lamented. "Shepherds and gamekeepers have affected its almost entire destruction, insomuch that it is doubtful if even a single breeding-place remains occupied. In the course of six weeks' excursions among the mountains, I saw only two individuals."

When given more adequate protection, the eagles flourished and increased their numbers. They, like most other creatures, have a fluctuating population in part related to the food supply. Deeside was good eagle country when, in the early 1960s, naturalists became aware that breeding in some parts of Scotland was being seriously affected by chlorinated hydrocarbon pesticides, used in sheep dips. For there are few sheep on Deeside.

A Deeside forester shattered me by describing the eagle as a sort of Highland vulture. It caught live prey—mountain hare, ptarmigan, fox cubs, young deer—but "generally it's a carrion-eater. One day I was out with a shepherd when we saw a golden eagle so stuffed with carrion from a deer carcass it couldn't fly. The eagle walked up a steep hillside!"

My binoculars must be rose-tinted. I could not think of the eagle as a North British vulture and preferred to recall it sweeping a hillside for live fare, trying to startle smaller creatures into incautious movements.

Circumstances have forced the golden eagle to be primarily a bird of the deer forest. It is protected by the law, but the law cannot be personally represented at every eyrie. A pair of eagles needs about ten square miles of country to sustain it and its young, with rather less ground if there is abundant food. One eagle territory might slightly overlap that of its neighbour.

Eagles gorge themselves on the unwanted gut from slain deer, which gives them a considerable supply of food, for gut accounts for about one-fifth of a deer's weight! The bounty provided by the grallochs is a major source of nourishment. If a stalker has to leave a gralloched stag on the hill overnight, he places beside it some object associated with man—a piece of silver paper, even a length of string—as a deterrent to natural predators.

At the end of a stalking season, the eagles can expect more bounty—more *grallochs*—during the hind-shooting season. There is good carrion in winter which, if severe, causes the deaths of the weakest deer. Then spring comes, and with it the red deer calves, many of which die. Of course, an eagle has to share the feasts with other scroungers—fox, crow and raven.

Eagles nesting in Deeside favour old pines. Some nests are built about ten feet from the crowns of the trees, where the strongest branches are to be found. Two eggs are laid, but often only one eaglet is reared. It may be that food is limited. The older, stronger eaglet takes more than its share of that brought to the eyrie; the other bird starves.

George Logan believes that the space available in a nest is an important factor. He knows a Scots pine where eagles nest, and here it was rare for both eaglets to reach independence. Then the pine was damaged by a winter gale, the foundations of the old eyrie spreading out. The nest had a circumference of six feet and in the first year of its extension both eaglets grew up and flew.

Have eagles a sense of fun? The stalker who watched three birds diving at some red hinds on the face of a crag believed they had. The hinds had to scatter. One of the fleeing hinds, incidentally, flushed a mountain hare, which began to run. An eagle pounced on the hare and carried it off.

The gushing river Ey provided a background sound during the trudge back to the main valley, and I motored on to the Linn o' Dee. The view opened up to reveal the Dee in frothy, noisy progress between belts of pine. Further on, the stillness of the day was being shattered by a hollow roar. The Dee, suddenly constricted between banks of schistose rock, formed the famous Linn. Above the Linn it was a typical Highland river, but for eighty yards it seemed to boil in a deep channel, with the rocks massed high on either side. At times they are festooned with icicles.

MacGillivray did not find the Linn of Dee interesting during his first visits. It consisted "merely of a pretty large stream dashing between rocks of no great height". Later he revised his judgement and the Linn seemed "very interesting". Yet he was not really enthusiastic. I usually avoid going to beauty spots, but the Linn appealed to me.

To Queen Victoria it was fascinating. She brought her family here for picnics, doubtless lecturing them about the dangers of walking too close to the edge of the cliffs. It is said that when Byron was a boy he scrambled down a declivity overhanging the fall, caught a lame foot on some heather and overbalanced. As he rolled towards certain death an attendant grabbed hold of him. Gwynn and Katie were less fortunate. A memorial stone records their deaths here in 1927.

The substantial bridge splits the interest. It was erected in 1857, before which "an Alpine wooden bridge" spanned the river thirty feet above the water, being washed away by the flood in 1829. Next year another wooden bridge was provided, to be replaced in due course by one of stone.

Wild Scotland lay above the Linn. Here one might trudge beside the water to the nurserylands of the Dee. Gibb and Hay noted that from the Linn "nature . . . has it nearly all to herself for many a long mile of mountain and glen". Pennant, staggering in from the hills after a walk from Blair Atholl, rejoiced when he saw trees around him again after being in the company of "naked summits, many of them topped with perpetual snow".

Out beyond the Linn of Dee went some patriotic men of Braemar with a grandiose plan. They proposed to cut a trench along which the river Tilt might be diverted, becoming a tributary of the Dee! George Wade, master road-builder, proposed to drive a road from Deeside to Speyside at a cost of £3,200, using cheap army labour. When I was in the Highlands local councils were still deliberating about the advisability of making such a road. Naturalists would be pleased if the scheme was forgotten.

The sight of heather, solitary pines, low hills glowering in winter purples and mauves, and high hills glistening with snow, prompted me to walk upriver to the White Bridge, at the junction of the Dee and Geldie. The Dee sweeps in from the north, passing through a pool called the Chest of Dee. Beyond the Chest is Glen Dee, in part dominated by the turret of the Devil's Point, 3,303 feet above sea level.

To find the source of the Dee one must climb to the speckled or brindled slope, which is the meaning in Gaelic from which the name Braeriarch is derived. Braeriarch, looming through cloud and mist to a height of 4,248 feet, is the second highest hill on the Cairngorm range.

The Dee has a boisterous childhood. It tumbles for about five hundred and fifty feet at Garrachory, and Hogg wrote of "the grisly cliffs which guard the infant rills of Highland Dee". Melting snow gives a roaring voice to the Dee, as a party who climbed by the fall in 1811 recalled.

> It was in flood at the time, from the melting of the snow and the late rains; and what was remarkable, an arch of snow covered the narrow glen from which it tumbled over the rocks. Here our landlord and our guide ascended the mountain by an easier, though more circuitous course; but I was determined not to lose sight of the river.
>
> We approached so near to the cateract as to know that there was no other lake or stream; and then we had to climb among huge rocks varying from one to ten tuns, and to catch hold of the stones or fragments that projected, while we ascended in an angle of 70 or 80 degrees.

The Dee is born on a platform about four thousand feet above the outflow of the river into the sea at Aberdeen.

8

WHEN FOXES MATE

The lean winter nights are for foxes. Once I stood on the road west of Braemar, with the frost so intense my ears were tingling, and heard the gruff, staccato barking of a hill fox in love—or whatever is the wild mammal's equivalent of love. Distance had softened the querulous "yap! yap! yap!" The sound seemed to be over in an instant and, in the quietness that followed, it was difficult to recall.

I was left in a dark, cold world, knowing that much was happening around me but having a prime irritation—I could not observe that life with the eyes. In winter, man sees only half of what is occurring in the Highlands.

The dog fox may have been responding to a sound I had not heard. The vixen usually screams an invitation. To us it might be simply an unpleasant but interesting sound—a blood-curdling scream, quivering, to die away on the still night air. It is enough to send a passionate dog fox into ecstasies of delight. The fox I heard could alternatively have reacted to an equally powerful impulse, having discovered the strong fresh scent of a vixen.

From the end of January into February, the love calls of the vixens, and the barking or yapping of the dog foxes, punctuate the Highland night. It is one time of the year when the normally taciturn dog fox finds a loud voice—and uses it. There is a parallel between a fox becoming vocal in midwinter and the red stag finding its voice on the rutting grounds in October, the 'month of the roaring'.

Do foxes bark at the moon, as some romantic writers and artists suggest? The moon is, of course, always portrayed full and low over the hills. The fox stands out in silhouette against a circlet of light. I have not seen a fox in the act of barking. Indeed, though I have raked about the hills in all hours of day and night, in all seasons of the year, I have not seen the fox with that sort of regularity that makes field study of the species worth-while. But some captive cubs inclined their heads downwards as they spoke.

Foxes move slyly through the long, dark nights, and sometimes we see them at first light, as the period of their greatest activity is ending. We hear them call—and in daylight, at snowtime, there is evidence of what they have been doing in the tracks and trails they have left behind.

If the presence of a vixen lures more than one male to the spot, fighting may occur. Being foxes, the contestants for the female's favours doubtless snarl and snap and seek dominant positions. Where nature is concerned, the fight will not be to the bitter end, which is wasteful. The inferior fox, weary or slightly injured, moves off.

The story of convergence and battle is told by tracks left in the snow, and dislodged tufts of hair—even flecks of blood—can testify to its severity. The late Richard Clapham, who frequented fox country for over forty years, wrote that two males in battle "spluttered and hissed like a bag full of Kilkenny cats".

The mating activity of foxes comes at a time when wild creatures are usually stupefied with cold, or simply desire to get enough food to keep them alive. There is, in any case, little surplus energy. Yet foxes trot lightly along the hill paths or through the high woods where foxy scents hang heavily on the air—a newspaper formed of vapour. Scent is left copiously by both dog and vixen.

In the world of the hill fox there always seems to be a preponderance of males, and so a vixen in breeding condition rarely remains unsatisfied. The unsuccessful suitors are occasionally flushed by man during the day as they sleep off their weariness in beds of ling or bracken or among some tumbled stones. A disturbed fox, streaking away, and keeping its fine brush above ground level, has a rich pelage that finds complementary tones in the countryside round about.

I have never set myself the task of watching foxes at an earth, but badgers have been great favourites, and foxes turned up at badger setts at that enchanting, grey time when it does not seem to be either day or night—the time when the country night shift begins. Visitors to the countryside expect too much when they 'clash around' on sunny afternoons. Dawn and dusk are the times to watch mammals.

I recall an evening when I reached the area of the badger sett about three hours before sundown in May, climbing a favourite tree and having a westerly wind to fan my face and keep my scent to a limited area. The tree grew on a hillside at about the same level as the sett. A badger taking a high path would (and very occasionally did) catch my scent.

This evening, before the striped head of the sow badger had appeared at the sett's capacious mouth, a fox came trotting along, stood for a moment on a knoll to look around, flicked its ears at any unusual sounds—even the grunts and squeak of a roding woodcock—and then sniffed around the sett. Before moving on, the fox had left its 'card', which would not please the generally tidier, more hygienically-disposed badger. Foxes may be unwelcome, smelly lodgers in the ramifications of a large sett.

Another time I came face to face with a grizzly veteran dog fox in one of the interminable rides criss-crossing a new conifer forest. The encounter was sudden, at a range of no more than twenty five yards. Momentarily I could admire the fox's splendid head, long slim muzzle, flattish 'mask' or face—and black nose, shining in its healthy moistness, with small silver highlights, not unlike an ultra-large blaeberry. The mind of a naturalist often retains such fine detail and misses—or forgets—some major points!

This fox seemed to disbelieve its eyes. Surely it had not allowed a man to approach so closely before taking evasive action. The action was not long delayed, and there was a streak of grey-brown as the animal went into the nearest tree cover. It was pointless to attempt to follow it.

A walker on hill or through a forest may pass through a cloud of musky fox tang. It is one of the most unpleasant of countryside flavours. It testifies that a fox has been present but the fox has slunk away, ensuring that it is not seen. The fox can itself smell strongly but it keenly scents other creatures at considerable distances. Perhaps this is one reason why it prefers, in its movements about the hill, to have the wind directly on its nose!

Foxes kept in captivity look forlorn. These energetic, vital creatures are not suited to pens. Fox cubs, taken young, are comparatively easy to rear. They make engaging pets—for a time. The last fox I saw in captivity had been reared, from being a cub, at a house on the periphery of a town. When excited the fox emitted a scent that nearly brought tears to the eyes of those standing nearby. It also had sharp claws which were kept sharp through scratching against furniture. It was banished from the house to a spare hen run.

During its time of recreation the fox could run at the end of a long chain. The hens in some of the adjoining runs must have tormented the fox. In a free-ranging state it would have become crazed at the sight of poultry, slaying far more birds than were needed to satisfy its hunger, as many disgruntled farmers know.

The fox wore a collar that had rubbed the hair from around its neck. Its brush, normally kept in an immaculate state, was strawy in colour and almost devoid of hair. Yet I could marvel, in close-up, at the rich brownish-red of the jacket in summer. There were greyish-white underparts to offset the jacket and, as an additional touch of artistry, black on the back of the ears and also the legs.

I prefer to see a hill fox bouncing along one of the upland paths. This feeling is not shared by the majority of Highlanders. To them a fox is a pest, and must die. A sheep farmer quivers with rage on finding the remains of a lamb near a fox earth, yet the lamb could have been taken as stillborn carrion. A keeper fears for the safety of his grouse and other game birds.

The owners of some Highland deer forests attempted to preserve the fox because it reduced the number of grouse, which when flushed might alert and panic the deer. An excited grouse has spoiled many a day's stalking on the hill. The fox, however, was capable of taking a deer calf in spring. The rabbit, a major item on the fox's menu, was hit by myxomatosis, but the fox is an opportunist and not at all fastidious in its choice of food. It takes whatever is toothsome and available—young deer, mountain hare, even the turkey-sized capercaillie of the pine forest. The remains of black grouse are found near the earths, and fox cubs may use a grouse wing as a plaything. These are the large items of food. The list of small stuff is almost endless. The fox even dines on black beetles infesting the upland trods in summer. Carrion is taken extensively in winter.

There are foxes in suburbia. They have their litters under tool sheds and knock the lids from dustbins in their nightly quest for food. Old men in hill country talk about a tougher type—'greyhound' foxes, the real hill breed that were few and far between and, when pursued were 'straight-necked', not deviating from a chosen direction, and running forever. Do any 'greyhounds' remain? Introductions of foxes have included Continental types. Lowland foxes were taken by sportsmen to hill areas. A Highland keeper I know speaks disparagingly of the lowland stock as "those wee red things"!

A fox on the hill is in the ever-fascinating world of red deer, ptarmigan, mountain hare and golden eagle. All are familiar to it through daily association, and all will appear on the fox's menu if it can get hold of them. A fox living near an eagle's eyrie might conceivably try for the eaglets or some of the food left lying around by the parent birds, but it has a respect for the eagle, which regularly lifts and kills fox cubs and has been known to dive on adults.

A hill fox couches on rock or heather or blaeberry. If left undisturbed, it stirs itself at sundown. The dark droppings (scats) of a fox are found in a variety of places and hold indigestible fragments of the food the animal has taken—fur, small bones, shiny beetle cases.

The fox trotting off for food, leaving a neat line of footings in the snow, is hard and wiry, rarely running to fat. If food is plentiful, some of it is buried, to be relocated with the assistance of the fox's ultra-keen scent.

A fox moving by day, as it is more inclined to do at mating time, is conspicuous in a world of white. The hills are layered with snow. Declining hours of daylight in autumn and early winter triggered off and sustained the processes by which other hill creatures—ptarmigan, mountain hare and stoat—assumed a covering of white. The snow buntings that move in twittering flocks across high ground are mainly white.

The end product of the fox's winter mating is the birth of cubs about April, a time when food is plentiful. The vixen, having enlarged a rabbit burrow or found a den in the rocks, dutifully stays with the offspring for the first week or so of their lives, subsisting on food brought in by the dog. Later both adult foxes comb the district for food. Around a fox earth is a strong tang of decay, cub droppings and rotting food. Maybe this is one reason why the vixen moves the cubs to other earths with such frequency.

Go near an earth containing cubs and you might hear the yap of the vixen warning her offspring of danger. One moment the cubs are frolicking at the mouth of the sett in the late sunshine; the next moment they are out of sight. Cubbing is part of the keeper's annual routine (once, indeed, some Highlanders made extra money by selling cubs at about 50p each).

Rarely, unpredictably, a keeper brings cubs home and keeps

them for a while. I saw five young cubs of a litter of seven. They bunched, staring, their ears rigidly alert, and when disturbed became hissing bundles covered with chocolate-brown hair, and showing the white of needle-sharp teeth. In the wild, these cubs had been fed on leverets and grouse, but in captivity they yielded, with equal enthusiasm, to chopped meat. The keeper tossed the corpse of an aged goose into the cage, and they demolished the bird in a spitting, scratching, biting, tugging fury. Even at three weeks old the cubs showed pronounced foxy features, right down to the white tip at the end of the tail.

Another keeper kept two well-grown foxes in an outhouse. Each fox wore a collar and, having been reared from cubs, they were accustomed to the man, who would lead them on a nightly visit to the local inn, where the foxes, shown to appreciative patrons, earned the man a few pints of ale. I visited those foxes after dark and, fumbling for a torch in the confined space, heard the sound of claws against plaster as the foxes tried to run up the walls!

As each cub reaches the stage of independence in the wild it tends to wander off. Many of the foxes killed in autumn are inexperienced young, not yet fully wise to the affairs of the world, having dispersed from the family groups. Winter provides a further test of their fortitude.

In good ground conditions a fox moves with a gliding action that carries it swiftly over the ground. While negotiating snow, however, it tends to use a mincing step. A large dog fox was seen to descend an ice-crusted drift in this way, meanwhile carrying its brush straight up in the air, compared with the ordinary position, almost horizontal, the tip inclined slightly towards the ground.

For the first three years of its life a fox continues to develop and gain weight. The prime of life is attained at about five years. In a hard environment, with every man's hand against it, the prospects of longevity appear poor, yet old and almost toothless foxes have been trapped or shot. They were in good condition. Age had weakened their powers, but they had developed greater cunning in obtaining food.

Few kind words have been spoken about the fox, this largest of our carnivorous land mammals, but I have not yet met a Highlander who despised the animal. There was always the element of respect for a sly, tough, adaptable animal which has triumphantly exploited all kinds of country.

I met an early tourist near Ballater in Deeside. We chatted about foxes. The visitor lived in a South Coast resort, and I wondered if he had ever seen a fox. He told me about a fox earth at the bottom of his long garden. The foxes were not normally a nuisance, "but they can be a bit noisy just after Christmas"!

F

9

FOREST OF MAR

The early morning air was keen but calm, mercifully lacking a cutting edge. A laggard sun banded upper Deeside with clear yellow light, imparting an illusion of warmth that was dispelled when my ear lobes and finger ends began to tingle. Standing near Mar Lodge, on the valley floor, I had a hunch that on such a day the conditions on the high Cairngorms, over two thousand feet higher, would be two coats warmer.

Overnight, rain swished across the slates of my lodgings at Braemar. Another inch or two of snow was heaped on the highest ground. The rain swept the atmosphere clear of haze and abated at dawn; now there was fiercely directional sunlight, with every detail of the landscape revealed with the clarity of the lines on a Victorian etching, only in full, rich colour.

My landlady—a naturalised Highlander—had lent me a copy of John Grant's *Legends of the Braes o' Mar*. Most of it was too fanciful, too prosy, for my taste, but Grant knew how to spin words and vary the pulse rate of the reader. His trouble was that he did not impart many hard facts.

I had read the book during the *forenicht*—the period between nightfall and bedtime, which Grant described as "a joyous, laughing, right merry time". He gave a cosy picture of peats blazing in a wide kitchen chimney; the "good wife" sitting on a low bench in her own cosy corner, "plying bravely the knitting

wires"; the men—"good men", naturally—gathering lore from
the newspapers or some venerable tome. To Grant, every
daughter was "blithe", and the one in this household operated
a spinning wheel.

My *forenicht* was spent reading, with a coal fire drenching
the room with heat, a television set flickering in the opposite
corner and the "good wife" darning socks!

I would have preferred to hear Grant tell a story. His little
book, with its genial generalisations, indicated that he had a
narrative skill best suited to the spoken word. "Long, long ago,"
he wrote, "wild and ferocious beasts roamed through the forests
of the Braes o' Mar—the wolf, the boar, the wild cat. They are
all away now, like the people with whom they contended for
possession, save a few cowed-down and spiritless wild cats."

The lady darning socks had, a few minutes before, directed
me to a feature in the day's newspaper which reported that the
wolf had returned to Badenoch, just over the Cairngorms, where
it was to be one of the exhibits in a wildlife park. The last wolf
in Scotland is believed to have been that slain near the Shenval
of Glengairn in the eighteenth century—a good two centuries
after the last wolf perished in England.

If John Grant had delved deeper into local records he might
have discovered that the wild boar (extinct in the wild state
since early in the seventeenth century) had been turned out in
the Forest of Mar in 1822. Two animals were released. A hunt
for boar was organised in the following October, and hounds
picked up the right scent. One boar was killed by gunshot, and
the remaining animal either pined or starved to death. A local
explanation was that there had been no acorns for it to eat.

I consulted William Scrope's book on deer-stalking. Mar, he
recorded, "consists of four contiguous glens on the north bank of
the Dee, with their various branches and ramifications, viz.
Glenquoich, Glenluie, Glendee and Glenguildy. It is bounded on
the north by Glenavon in Banffshire, and the hills of
Rothiemurchus and Glenfeshie in Inverness-shire; on the west
by part of the forest of Atholl and the glen of Baynock; on the

south by the river Dee; and on the east by part of the forest of
Invercauld."

The story of this large, outstanding deer forest is also, in good
measure, the story of Highland hunting, every phase of which
can be well illustrated from the records. There were royal spectators in the early days. In the eleventh century, King Malcolm
took time off to watch the slaying of the red deer. Queen Mary,
in the sixteenth century, gloried in the deer drive organised for
her pleasure. Mary arrived in Mar during 1563.

The records state that two thousand burly Highlanders
encircled and drove two thousand stags, plus "roes, does and
other game". (Round figures in old accounts might be taken
with a pinch of salt). At dusk that day 360 deer had been slain,
with "five wolves and some roes". If 2,000 deer had been driven
into a constricted area, the men who assembled with bows and
firearms must either have been few in number or poor shots.

The death of the stags was not the only excitement on this
occasion. A number of deer, half-crazed no doubt, charged a
line of beaters. These men considered that the best way of
escaping was to lie on the ground, but several were trampled to
death and others could only hobble away.

A hunting extravaganza early in the seventeenth century
was attended by John Taylor, of London. He was indifferently
housed by the Earl of Mar but received plenty of food, including
"moor-fresh salmon, heather-cocks, caperkellies, termagents".
The "moor-fresh salmon" were presumably lifted from the headwaters of the burns, where the fish had hoped to spawn. The
other creatures noted were, in modern spelling, red grouse,
capercaillie and ptarmigan. They are still represented in the
fauna at Mar. Wrote an exuberant John Taylor: "All these,
and more than these, we had continuously, in superfluous
abundance."

Rounding up the deer began early in the morning. Over five
hundred disciplined men spread out across the hills and drove in
the herds—"two, three or four hundred in a hearde"—to
appointed places and "then when the day is come the lords and

gentlemen of their companies doe ride or go to the said places, sometimes wading up to the middles through burnes and rivers".

The guests lay on the ground "till those foresaid scouts, which are called the tinckell, doe bring down the deere. . . . After we had stayed three hours or thereabouts, we might perceive the deere appeare on the hills round about us (their heads making a shew like a wood) which being followed close by the tinckell are chased down in to the valley where we lay." At the crucial moment, a hundred couple of strong Irish greyhounds were loosed. The weapons held by the men were "gunnes, arrowes, durks and daggers" and in two hours eighty deer had been slaughtered. August was the traditional time for such sport, for it did not interrupt the harvest. That August, Ben Avon had "a furred mist upon his snowy head instead of a nightcap".

Men from various walks of life assembled, but there was some conformation in dress—blue flat caps, kerchief around the neck, no breeches "but a jerkin of the same stuff that their hose is of, their garters being bands or wreaths of hay or straw, with a plaid about their shoulders, which is a mantle of divers colours, of much finer and lighter stuff than their hose". In his reference to the substitute for breeches, Taylor was describing the kilt!

A record of this form of Scottish hunting—the encirclement of an area and the driving of its wild beasts, mainly deer, to selected places for slaughter—was left by a Rev. Dr Robertson in 1799. "The natives hunted the deer by surrounding them with men, or by making large enclosures of such a height as the deer could not overlap, fenced with stakes and intertwined with brushwood," he observed.

"Vast multitudes of men were collected on hunting days who, forming a ring round the deer, drove them into these enclosures, which were open on one side. From some eminence which over-looked the enclosure the principal personages and others who did not choose to engage in the chase were spectators of the whole diversion. The enclosures were called, in the language of the country, elerig."

A tinchell had its own code of conduct. No-one had to fire a gun or pistol during the event. The landowner must be present before a deer was *gralloched*. Neither drunkenness nor swearing was permitted.

Was it just for sport? Or were the crafty lairds—devout Scotsmen all—conducting the forerunner of the British Army's 'autumn manœuvres'? A large body of men, well-disciplined, went through co-ordinated actions in rough country that led to a prescribed end: the encirclement and rout of deer. Such tactics, with slight modification, might be used in warfare.

One of the last great hunts in the Forest of Mar undoubtedly had a political significance. It took place in 1715 and the Earl had invited nearly eight hundred guests, most of them being well-connected socially. For a time the chase was their delight. Then they assembled in solemn mood and heard proposals for a rising in support of the Jacobite cause. The Earl had probably looked very critically at the efforts made by the men summoned to round up the deer. How would they fare against the English?

In 1769, when Thomas Pennant visited Mar, the flamboyance had gone from local hunting—indeed, it had left local life, for the tragedy of Culloden had occurred. The Jacobite cause was smashed. Great social changes were under way. Men told Pennant of the days of "unmatchable hunting" and pointed out that English troops still formed a garrison in Braemar Castle.

Most modern visitors to Deeside cross the Cairnwell or travel up the valley from the coast. Pennant arrived on foot from the west, having travelled up the Tilt from Atholl. In his progress across the bare lands he noticed red deer, roe deer and black grouse. "The tops of the hills swarmed with grouse and ptarmigan." Pennant's list of birds included lapwing, whimbrel (could it have been the curlew?) and dotterel. Hawks were common. Anyone who destroyed an eagle received, in the modern term, 12½p. and there was 5p. for a dead peregrine, goshawk or hooded crow. The ravenous local foxes fed on "roes, sheep and even the goats".

Slowly, after the Jacobite troubles, the Mar estate recovered part of its lost grandeur. There was, indeed, a hankering for the glory of the past in 1850, when Queen Victoria and Prince Albert were promised a deer drive. The deer cannot have remained temperamentally suited to being herded in the mass, for that is all we hear about it.

At Mar—and, indeed, at Atholl, just over the hills—a variety of wildlife introductions took place. When reindeer were released they were soon made extinct by Highland conditions. Or maybe the wrong type of reindeer was being used. Some English park stags were kept in a special enclosure in 1884, and were introduced to hinds brought in from the forest. The deer mated, but when their offspring were turned loose they did not long survive.

Stalking was in fashion. Its early publicist, Scrope, mentioned the attractions of getting *quiet shots*. No longer were deer driven to passes, or coursed with dogs, except when they were wounded. The little disturbance which stalking occasioned to the forest "keeps the deer from wandering, though the sport is of less brilliant description".

Deerhounds were no longer being generally used. Charles St John (who preferred stalking to "running red-deer with the rough deer-hound") wrote flatteringly about the hound's intelligence. "Many deer-hounds have a wonderful instinct in singling out the biggest head of horns in a herd of deer, and in sticking to this one, regardless of the rest of the herd." Yet "it will often happen that the dogs set off after some hind or young stag, who leads both them and you away a long chace, unsatisfactory both in its commencement and termination, disturbing the ground and taking up twice as much time as would be required to kill the fine old ten-antlered stag whose head you covet for your lobby, and whose haunches you wish to send to your English friend to show him what size a mountain-fed stag will grow to".

Mar is lovely still. I stood near Mar Lodge on that crisp, clear winter day when the roadway was barred by shadows thrown by the Scots pine. One tree soared with the smooth tapering elegance of a ship's mast for fifty feet and more before burgeoning. Its lower branches had been cast, and the upper branches, from which the bark had peeled, were golden.

A coal tit rummaged for food among the greenery. Through the air came the chatter of a peregrine falcon, which caused an instant switch of attention. A day or two before, while walking near some crags lower down Deeside in a blustering wind I watched a falcon above the crest of the hill. When it was visible, the bird's distinctive scimitar wings were partly closed, and the whole bird was in silhouette. It lay on the wind. Sometimes the falcon was obscured by the ragged edges of low cloud.

The falcon I now saw circled low in sunlight, and its calling must have been heard a mile away. Peregrines, glamour birds in the Highlands, are as common on Deeside as in any part of Britain and here, as elsewhere, the species is mainly a pigeon-eater. A local naturalist told me that the smaller pigeons (racers and stock doves) are preferred to the hefty woodpigeons which have proliferated in the age of State forests. A peregrine strikes down a variety of birds when stooping on prey, attaining over one hundred miles an hour before the impact occurs.

'Blue sleeves', as Scotsmen used to call it, does not always succeed in killing. I have watched the peregrine miss several chances. Once I was partly to blame, for my presence in the district held its attention. Half a dozen pigeons flew by, using an old migration route near which the peregrines nested. The peregrine set off in pursuit but had not attained great height when the pigeons became aware of the lean blue figure pursuing them. Those pigeons dropped as though they had been suspended from the sky—and someone cut the string!

Mar Lodge is not what one would expect to see in the Highlands, where the architecture remembered best is that lovely fusion of the Scottish and French. Mar Lodge, which is immense, has an Elizabethan style and Edwardian decor. The walls are of warm pink granite and there is half-timbering on the gables and the overhanging eaves. Red slates were used for the roof.

The Duke of Fife and his wife—daughter of the future Edward VII—had the place built when an older Lodge was

Highland fox sniffing the breeze

Highland garron

1848 VICTORIA 1848

(*opposite*) The Linn of Dee, showing a bridge that was new when
Queen Victoria came this way (*above*) Bridge leading to Mar Lodge

Mountain hares in winter coat

destroyed. An experienced architect was employed but the Princess Royal drew the first rough sketch of the form it had to take and she concerned herself with much of the detail, even stipulating the wallpaper design and selecting curtains to be draped in the bedrooms of the domestic staff. When Queen Victoria was holidaymaking in Deeside in the autumn of 1895 she was prevailed upon to lay the foundation stone, which she would do with experienced ease. The splendid new Mar Lodge was ready for occupation in the summer of 1898.

The rooms within cannot have changed much since the opulent 1890s, with walls adorned by two hundred mounted deer heads, each head having an inscription that gives the details of the kill—the sportsman concerned, place of execution and the date. The Prince of Wales, a visitor to old Mar Lodge about 1820, shot some of the heads which are now displayed.

If the array of heads within Mar Lodge is impressive, that seen in the detached ballroom is staggering in its number and pattern. The underside of the roof, the beams and upper walls, are festooned with heads, just over three thousand of them, dating mainly to the period between 1860 and 1870. The Duke of Fife held a world record, about four thousand, for the number of deer he stalked and shot. Heads set out in the ballroom are among the best of the collection. No good heads have been shot in modern times, for the policy has been to upgrade the stock. The factor told me that, indeed, only four heads had been added to the collection during the past decade.

Mar Lodge might have become a winter sports centre. In the early 1960s ski slopes were laid out on Creag Bhalg, tows were installed and there was even equipment to produce artificial snow. The plans foundered when the slopes above the lodge were found not to hold snow for long. Mar Lodge now caters for guests on sporting holidays. On the estate are fifty miles of private roads and tracks and the pursuits include stalking, grouse-shooting and fly-fishing for salmon.

The factor said that this 66,000-acre estate held, at that moment, over one thousand stags, and the forest took in Ben

Macdhui, which is not only the second highest hill in Scotland but also happens to be the county boundary between Inverness and Aberdeenshire.

The term 'factor' interested me. It is not used, to my knowledge, in England, and factor is not specifically a deer forest term. It is applied to a man who manages an enterprise. In this case I spoke to an estate factor, who in Scotland has always been a resident agent. The owners of deer forests hire out the sporting rights for a season, or for part of a season. The charge made depends on the nature of the forest and also the degree of extra facility provided—lodge, stalker, transport.

Many Highland stalkers are also small-time sheep farmers, or they undertake extra duties, some of them by the rivers, ensuring that all those who fish have the necessary licences.

10

DERRY LODGE

A group of red-roofed buildings lay just off the road north of the river between Linn of Dee and Quoich. I waited here in joyful anticipation of one of the special sights of a Highland winter—the feeding of red deer stags.

About twenty young stags were assembled for a late break-fast. They moved tensely across grassland that had been cropped so well it looked as fine as a bowling green. In due course the deer relaxed a little or kept a watching brief on the road along which the rations would be brought.

The heads of these Mar stags were elegant, symmetrical. I could not help but see the animals gathered on the greensward, which was light green in colour, uniform in tone. Against it the deer stood out, the thick, greyish coats toning best with the landscape of the lower hills on which many of them lie out during the short winter days. Food, not curiosity, brings them down to the edge of the road.

A stag delicately scratched its jaw with a rear foot. Lifting the hind leg it stretched it forward to meet the head, the animal's neck having bent with the elasticity of rubber. Leg and jaw met in a brief, delicate period of rubbing. Later the stag turned its head again to lick and nuzzle its side. The disturbed hair was thick and rather tattered. Generally, the deer's coat resembled an old army blanket!

Displacement activity occurred when two stags met head to head, with interlocked horns, and engaged in a short pushing match. Through it some nervous energy could be released in a tense situation. Not knowing quite what to do in the circumstances, they turned to mock conflict. Other deer emulated them, and I heard the dry rattle of antlers. Some stags, lying down, solemnly chewed the cud. I noticed a variation of tone from one deer to another, for which the light was partly responsible. The tone changed subtly as the animals moved around.

A stag defecated, and large chunky droppings spread across the turf, adding to the ground a little of the fertility it had lost through the deer's grazing. A jet aircraft passed with a sound like a thunderclap. It was accepted by the deer as something normal, but a red grouse called irritably from up the hillside.

The feeding party—two jovial men—arrived in a vehicle of four-wheel drive, behind which bounced a trailer laden with good clover hay, potatoes and deer cobs. The stags had been fed daily since January, when the weather entered its chilliest phase. The driver sounded the vehicle's horn—a series of lively toots— and a movement of deer down the wooded hillside quickened. Many animals had been holding back among the trees and I had not realised how big was the throng.

Clambering into the trailer I was driven towards the stags in comfort, couched on hay. We passed the remains of a salt lick which (said one of the feeding party) was the second to have been put out for the deer within two months. Vehicle and trailer lurched over ground that was rougher than it looked. Tyres bit through the grass into soft earth, which looked peaty.

Though eager for food, the deer kept an acceptable distance from us. Many of their wild instincts remained. The beauty of the morning would be lost to the deer, whose sight is believed to be monochromatic. (In any case, they would be happiest in the half light of dawn and dusk.) Beyond the verdant green near the buildings the wilderness began with tousled ground, orange and yellow in hue, and an odd birch tree. Beyond were Scots pines and snow-capped hills. The red roofs of the buildings near the road added a splash of primary colour to a panoramic view that included the valley of the Dee.

The feeding party departed for Derry Lodge. I followed on foot, passing a gate on which a notice had been posted urging visitors not to climb the hills during the stag-stalking season, which extends from 1st August to 20th October.

Lui Water drains the glen in which Derry Lodge stands. It was clearly a river in a hurry, at times having the strength to roll along huge grey boulders or to bite deeply into its low banks. I looked beyond the Lui to natural pinewood of the most pleasurable kind—the sort of self-regenerating area of pines and their attendants that Ptolemy had in mind when, in the second century, he thought up the title 'Caledonian Forest'. These pines regularly broadcast seed, but of the many seedlings that grow, most have their growth checked by browsing deer. It happens particularly when there are too many deer for the land. Part of the skill of a stalker is to ensure that the animals are not so numerous they begin to eat themselves out of house and home.

MacGillivray did not think that Highland deer ate enough! Writing in the middle of last century, before the deer population had climbed to its peak, he pointed out that the red deer preferred to graze the richest pastures. When they had access to them they neglected the hill grass. "I was surprised to see the often luxuriant green and succulent pasture of the corries perfect, without the least appearance of ever having been touched by an animal. On the moors and hills also, even in the woods, and in most cases in the valleys and haughs, the pasturage seemed quite entire and luxuriant. It is evident, therefore, that a great deal of cattle-food annually runs to waste; and that what the Deer have untouched would suffice to feed a vast number of Sheep, Goats and Cattle."

A young plantation of massed conifers on the western bank of Lui Water illustrated man's modern approach to timber production. It was gloomy within. The mass of trees prevented strong light from reaching the ground, leading to a sterile appearance—just a faded carpet of cast needles. Breaking out of the shadowy calm near yet another Deeside linn I looked across the water at the old forest. It looked gay by comparison.

The next wood to be seen was more open and potentially more interesting. A party of roe deer skipped away. The animals were dark, of the old British type no doubt, if anything smaller than roe found in the more favourable country south of the Highland line. In Perthshire, for instance, the roebucks have consistently larger horns.

My group of deer consisted of a doe, its well-grown youngster (the twin might have perished) and a young buck in velvet, which I took to be one of the offspring of the year before. The doe was probably carrying young, though as yet they were in an early stage of development. A doe mated in August does not give birth to her fawns until the following May or June. The fertilized ovum is not implanted in the wall of the uterus until about late December. The doe thus carries young in the course of development for five months or so.

Yearlings stay with the does until the female comes back into season, when the young bucks are chased away. They wander through established territories—where they are chased off by resident bucks—and either find niches of their own or perish. The mortality of inexperienced, disorientated yearlings is high.

Glen Lui widened. Another mass of young conifers sat smugly behind deer fencing. Old pinewoods adorned the slopes, and within them (I had been told) were capercaillie, birds that spend their winter days feeding on pine needles, steadily losing weight, which they regain in spring. By planting young conifers, man actually provides the local capercaillie with tenderer fare than they would otherwise have had!

On the right-hand side of the glen was a sweeping heathered hillside, extending high and far off. To the left of the track the land slipped away to where the river tinkled over stones and shingle. There were grassy fields in the bottom of the valley, and here and there the foundations of former buildings. Before sheep farming, or the management of deer for stalking, became dominant occupations in the Highlands a considerable human population lived between the high hills. They were displaced. Redundancy is not modern.

Almost straight ahead lay the untidy bulk of Sgor Dubh (2,432 feet) and Carn Crom, 400 feet higher and the guardian of the upper glen. The first ray of the midsummer sun is said to strike a hollow on Carn Crom in which a crock of gold is buried! The snow lay like grey poultices across the tops of the hills. Patches of snow streaked the heather to the east of the glen, and more flurries descended to join them. The day that started out brightly and calmly was now dull. Cloud was being wafted in by a moderate breeze.

Just before the cloud canopy was complete, shafts of sunlight broke through to sweep the glen like theatre spotlights. Seen against the grey washes of indeterminate cloud, the sunlight was silvery but it came to earth in a tangle of dun-coloured vegetation and appeared to glow. A beam of light traversed the eastern slope and alighted on a group of over one hundred stags lying in rank heather.

For maybe a minute the deer stood out because each antler was rimmed by sunlight. It was possible to examine a fourteen-pointer stag so easily that I began to wonder if this animal was not a fifteen-pointer. A 'wee bump' adorned one horn in addition to the tines. The bump could be counted as a tine if a key ring could be hung upon it. As the stag would not permit this classical experiment to occur I was left pondering on whether the bump was a tine or merely an 'offering'.

Red deer had crossed the track that day, as indicated by fresh droppings and many slots. I did not need to be a detective to judge why this had occurred. The vehicle of the feeding party had wiped its feet on the grassland west of the track—a vehicle that was now returning with an empty trailer after the morning's mercy run.

The glen's moment of national fame came a few months before the 1914–18 war erupted. A lost Zeppelin appeared. The bemused crew stared into the blackness of a Highland night. They dropped a flare, which spluttered on the slope of Sgor Dubh.

Derry Lodge looked primly Victorian. Windows had been temporarily boarded up, and the effect was of a creature with several eyeless sockets. The austerity of the Lodge's setting near the head of the glen was tempered by stands of young pines that were upstarts compared with the giants beyond, whose roots jostled each other, weirdly contorted, before dipping into the peaty ground. Equally gnarled and twisted branches supported a latticework of branches and dark needles. Through chinks in the foliage, and between branches extending outwards almost in an expression of despair, I saw hills capped with snow that was being replenished by fresh falls even as I watched. Eddies of the storm could be felt deep in the glen.

I amused myself, while sitting on a pine root, by repeopling the glen, drawing together the strands of its story with the help of a few facts and much imagination. The Caledonian Forest ran well up the hills and must have overawed the first of the settlers by its vastness. I had seen the remains of buildings. Once they were thatched to turn the weather. Within them unnumbered, unremembered generations of simple, dour folk lived, loved and died.

Townsfolk came to the country not for pleasure but for profit. There was wealth in the upstanding pines and other trees. Man had been slowly denuding the Highlands for years, but fellings that began in the seventeenth century changed the appearance of the district radically and at great speed. Hundreds of pines creaked, squealed and fell. Their trunks were cleaned up and moved to the mill at the mouth of Glen Quoich, a near neighbour of the Lui, or they were consigned to the sea by the river at floodtime. These remote pines had been safe for years because of the cost of transportation, but ingenious man devised a system of forming trunks into rafts and moving them by water. The system was developed, and reached its greatest use and refinement on the Spey.

A writer of the eighteenth century perceived: "When the river is swelled with rains, great floats of timber are sent down into the low countries." Six guineas was the cost of a tree from eighty to 90 feet in height and four and a half feet in diameter at the lower end. It had taken nature several hundred years to grow it.

By 1884 (when Gibb and Hay trudged through Deeside) some of the consequences of commercial exploitation were clear to see; "all around us now are the sad-looking remains of the once noble Forest of Mar. The fine trees, for which it was at one time so famous, have nearly all disappeared—carried down by the river to serve mercantile purposes." The area had been "stripped of its trees by the same influence that is losing to the Gael his much-cherished mother tongue".

Other influences were now at work. Dredging operations had been undertaken in the stream near Derry Lodge. Heaps of displaced shingle lay beside it, and might tempt the oystercatchers that would come flying up the river in March looking for nesting sites. A young man was undertaking some modest reclamation work of his own, examining the debris by the river for semi-precious stones washed down from the hill. Looking for them here, he said, was a convenient alternative to seeking a vein of gemstones on high ground.

Two walkers appeared, striding briskly from the cover of the pines. They had walked through the Lairig Ghru, the famous pass between Aviemore and Braemar. The distance between those two points is 27 miles, and 10 miles of walking remained to them before they would see the main street of Braemar. Victorian walkers were urged by one writer to remove collars and cuffs (if men) or "kilt their skirts" (if women).

The Victorians were ever ready to take advice from writers. Advice was at least freely offered on a variety of topics. John Colquhoun outlined a few rules useful to a hill-climber:

> . . . if he would escape the suppressed smile of derision which his flagging will be sure to excite from the sturdy hillman who carries

G

his bag. One is—to eat a very little breakfast; another, to drink as little as possible, but especially no spirits and water. If you can hold out without drinking till your luncheon—or dinner-time—your thirst will never be more oppressive; but once begin, and the difficulty of passing a clear brook is very much increased.

The provision-basket should only consist of a cold fowl or a few sandwiches, and a bottle of table-beer or light ale. When you again begin your exertions, make your attendant carry a bottle of strong tea, without cream or sugar, which will more effectually quench your thirst than a whole flaskful of spirits and water to correspond. Should any object to this *tea-total* system, a little fruit may be no bad substitute.

When I first took out a licence, I thought the spirit-flask almost as indispensable as the powder flask; but experience has since taught me that nothing more effectually expends the remaining strength of the half-worn-out sportsman than a few pulls at the liquor-flask, however diluted : he gains a temporary stimulus, which soon ends in complete exhaustion !

It was late in the afternoon when I returned to Derry Lodge. I took cover behind a pine tree, having seen a young stag appear. The deer was advancing with frequent pauses to yet another feeding area. Other deer were bounding down the hill, then standing to look around them, though in fact they seemed to be operating mainly on the evidence of their ears. All the deer were young animals, with the exception of a senior citizen with ten points and an old warrior that had lost its left antler. Had the missing horn been left on the hill during the fury of the October rut? Twenty-six stags were arrayed before me. Two of them interlocked their antlers and briefly sparred eighty yards from where I stood.

In my home area, where I watch sika deer, there is always much sparring of a gentle kind just before the casting of horn takes place. Is this behaviour, and the occasional frenzy of stags that suddenly have a whim to run desperately about a field, related to hormonal changes? The big stags cast first, and when an old boy is without antlers at a time when younger animals are still arrayed he maintains a dominance of a sort by rearing on hind legs to spar with the forelegs.

If there had been no stags in sight near Derry Lodge I would have been aware of their presence. A number of Scots pines had been rubbed. In one case, where a substantial branch had sprung up from near the base of a young pine, rubbing had been so brisk that the white wood was exposed. On the main trunk only the dark scales of the bark were missing, leaving the tree at this point with a reddish hue. These stags were not the animals I had seen earlier, for in my walk down the glen I saw the original herd still spread about the open moor.

I had to go to Quoich if only to hear a local person pronounce the name. Here is a long, deep glen with an assembly of old pines. The glen runs up towards the 'hill of the table', or Beinn a' Bhuird, an ascent of which offers a stiffish climb to a walker and an exciting motor run to those fortunate enough to be able to use the estate road which, in almost five miles, rises to over 3,600 feet, ending a few hundred feet from the summit plateau. Nowhere in Britain can vehicles climb higher while remaining on a track.

I have not traversed the Beinn a' Bhuird road but have been told that by and large the gradients are not severe. The surface is of durable grit. I was fascinated by the thought of being able to motor in minutes, in winter, from the glen of the pines to the sterility of the high Cairngorms. Up there, winds moan over a desert of granite blocks and heather. Snowdrifts assume futuristic shapes or hang ominously in the form of gigantic cornices extending the hill's profile. It can be chilly even in summer. Pennant, visiting a small loch under Beinn a' Bhuird in 1769, was told that ice had been seen at the end of July!

Quoich is Gaelic for cup. The cup is a circular depression in a big rock by the river, which has been responsible for its erosion. The cup near the Linn of Quoich is also known as the Earl of Mar's Punchbowl. I could have walked to it in five minutes from the end of the motor road, but this would have been foolish with so much to see. Quoich hardly qualifies as a hamlet, but there was the brilliant red roof of a cottage, home of the stalker who for years lived at Derry Lodge, and—excitingly—a gathering of stags near the back door. The deer were clearly accustomed to being fed.

The roof screamed to be noticed. It had not yet been toned down a few shades by Highland weather. The deer did not want to be noticed. They moved off, but not far, crossing the little river and eyeing me slyly from thick cover on the other side.

I walked between pines and—on a sunny afternoon—actually felt a winged insect settle on my face. The bridge spanning the Quoich, and also providing a vantage point for the Linn, was a substantial structure. It took only seconds to locate the Earl of Mar's Punchbowl, which once held water—or whatever the good Earl arranged to put in it. When he entertained hundreds of distinguished Highlanders who became absorbed by talk of rebellion in August 1715, it was reported that "ankers of potent Aquavitae" went into the hole. The water that carved out a bowl could not leave its work alone and has now eroded away the base.

The Earl of Mar was not an unsophisticated rustic. He had poise, being active in national politics and attaining, during the reign of Queen Anne, the rank of Secretary of State for Scotland. He was disgruntled at the time he brought the local lairds to Quoich, having been dismissed from his government post when George I came to the throne. So there was a personal as well as a Scottish reason why he would wish the Stuarts to be restored.

The Jacobites rallied and raised their standard at Braemar, the spirit of the time being caught by this verse:

> The standard on the Braes o' Mar
> Is up and streaming rarely;
> The gathering pipe on Lochnagar
> Is sounding lang an' sairly.
> The Highland men,
> Frae hill and glen,
> In martial hue,

Wi' bonnets blue,
Wi' belted plaids,
An' burnished blades,
Are coming late and early.

The Linn of Quoich, once the setting for intrigue, is now a
'beauty spot'. Beyond the Punchbowl are tumbled pines, among
them rotted trees that supposedly fell during the gale that
wrecked the Tay railway bridge. Deer use standing timber as
rubbing posts. They seem to ignore the hills of black ants, which
would have been irresistible to some woodland deer I know
in Westmorland.

I had a strong urge, on the return to Linn of Dee, to scan the
hillside to the right of the road. This hill had once been covered
by scrub, now clear-felled, leaving innumerable grey stumps, as
unsightly as rotten teeth until some replanting scheme took
place. Each stump trailed grey roots or extended small grey
branches. The hillside also had patches of scree, jumbles of
coarse grass—and a little heather.

Four red stags were grazing high on the slope. I caught sight
of them through binoculars. The sunlight rimmed them or I
might not have picked them out. About twenty yards away—
and now so conspicuous I felt foolish at not having seen them
before—lay a large group of stags. Their upsoaring antlers
looked like a mini-forest.

The stags watched me at a range of about two hundred yards,
looking as ancient as the grey rocks and the grey tree stumps
around them.

11

WIDE-AWAKE HARES

Late evening, on the road to Tomintoul. I expected a sudden transition from daylight to darkness, as though someone had switched off a light. Yet here was a lingering afterglow that would have done justice to an evening in May. The Cairngorms, spread for miles across the western skyline, had an aura of soft pink. Because the air was still, the cold was bearable.

The surface of the road lay at over one thousand five hundred feet above sea level—about five hundred feet higher than Braemar, which I had left a short time before. The road had broken out of the bondage of walls and fencing, and now nothing substantial lay between me and the heatherlands on either side.

Into view—not more than twenty yards away—lolloped a mountain hare, and its fur looked entirely white. *Lepus timidus* is well-known even to those who have not seen it alive because of accounts frequently given of its habit of assuming a white coat to match the winter snow. In fact, a minority of Scottish mountain hares go completely white. The animal I saw was, as far as I could judge, one of the minority.

The hare progressed for a few yards in that ungainly way of the species when operating in bottom gear. The animal's long hind legs, adapted for rapid and powerful propulsion, serve best when there is rising ground and the pace is keen. The hare raised its black-tipped ears and tuned them in to the local wave-lengths. The only sounds on this still and cold evening were probably those made by itself. I have rarely known the world to be so quiet.

The hare surveyed the area with all the caution that centuries of predation by eagles and foxes have bred in the tribe. It reared up to take a broader view of the world, and then went into a nervous face-washing routine. The nostrils twitched. Had the hare received a faint reek of car exhaust fumes? Slowly the hare relaxed and set its chisel teeth to work on heather that looked less appetising than boot laces.

In midwinter the ling provides little more than 'fill belly' for the mountain hare, yet there is little else to eat at this elevation. Raymond Hewson studied the mountain hare in Banffshire with great dedication, and he examined the stomach contents of hares collected in each month of the year. Ling formed 90 per cent of the winter and 50 per cent of the summer food, a significant alternative to ling being cotton-grass. When the winter takes a savage turn, and the moors are blanketed with snow, many hares migrate to lower land. It is then that you might see them moving about the high glens.

Picture, then, a whitish hare on an almost black moor. It is a sight I find continuously interesting, for most of my experiences of hares have been with the common brown variety of the low-lands. My first intimation of the presence of a brown hare is when it bursts from a tuft of rushes or from wizened litter on a woodland floor. The hare departs at speed, leaving behind a compact area of flattened, still warm vegetation where it has been lazing away the daytime hours. Hares, like most shy mammals, feed mainly at dawn and dusk.

Spending its life on the surface of the ground, unlike the deep-burrowing rabbit, the hare long since developed the knack of being unobtrusive. If it is caught out in the open on early spring days when the ground is as bare as a billiard table, it snuggles down until from a distance it resembles a clod of earth. In thicker vegetation, it is virtually undetectable. A poacher boasted he could detect a hare in its 'form' by the sparkle in the animal's eye, which is beyond my abilities. I believed him, however, for he once by the same stratagem showed me a crouching woodcock.

Disturb a hare, and it will outpace most predators. If it has a weakness it is that of keeping slavishly to certain runs. Poachers know to within a few inches where they should place their nets. And thousands of years of evolution counted for nothing when upstart man devised the motor car and began to travel about at night with headlamps blazing. Such light throws a hare into confusion. Its eyes glow back redly as it dashes wildly to and fro across the road. Many hares are knocked down and killed, and at daybreak the mashed bodies provide a tasty breakfast for the crows.

One blustery day I walked to within eight feet of a hare that lay in its 'form' but the wind was in my favour. A hare encountered as it feeds in the half light may rear up, long ears upstretched, nostrils flickering, but if seen at closer quarters it crouches, ears draped along its back, the bright eyes gleaming from within circlets of fawn hair. Stare fixedly at such a hare and it often remains 'frozen' for a long time. The animal waits for your concentration to fail. Look away, and the brown hare departs, accelerating furiously.

I saw twenty-five hares feeding on re-seeded land one evening in early spring when this tract had freshed up ahead of the neighbouring fields. A farmer with a large population of hares shot off some off them at night by firing down the headlamp beams from his vehicle. With him I watched groups of hares feeding. Occasionally, two animals would become restive, dash around each other, rear on their hindlegs and 'box' with their forefeet; then the grazing was resumed. It was in March—and in low country—the time when hares are 'mad'. By this time many hares have gone through the courtship ritual, and there are leverets to be found. A female going to its nursery 'form' to suckle its young gave a tremendous bound when the 'form' was near so that the scent trail was broken.

Near Braemar : a rubbing post used by red deer

View across Deeside looking towards Quoich

(*overleaf*) Pine trees near Quoich in the upper Dee

Leverets, unlike young rabbits, are born with their bodies covered with hair. Their eyes are open, and the creatures have the ability to move around at an early age. The female usually distributes its family around the area to lessen the risk of the whole family perishing. I found one leveret when there were several inches of snow. The wee creature had broken its statuesque pose in the 'form' and was now terribly vulnerable. Brown-grey pelage, flecked with lighter hairs, stood out against the glistening snowfield. As the leveret moved it would leave a scent trail that predators could follow.

That leveret was anxious because there was a weasel not far away, and the weasel had already lacerated one of its ears. Intent on its prey, the weasel did not notice me until I was only about twelve feet away, and then it escaped by diving into a snowdrift near a stream, giving the leveret some temporary relief from torment.

The mountain hare to be found in Highland Scotland is a different species. Like the brown hare it is a surface-dweller and therefore needs to be wide-awake to escape the attention of predators. In Scotland, the mountain hare is taken as food by a variety of birds and beasts, including the golden eagle.

Seeing the white hare on an almost black moor above Deeside, I was tempted to think that nature had erred. As the day waned, the moorland became darker—and the hare lighter. It moved nowhere near the few patches of snow, against which a benign nature had arranged for it to be camouflaged. Snow melted early from the moor that winter and was not replenished by further heavy falls. The hare remained white.

In summer plumage, the hare I saw might have been taken to be a large rabbit, being stockier, smaller, than the brown hare of the lowlands. The mountain type's ears looked shorter, more rounded, than those of its low country cousin.

As I watched it, a short-eared owl flew by, looking like a big brown moth. The owl's head turned and its brilliant, unblinking eyes took in more ground. It undoubtedly saw the hare but it ignored a creature of greater bulk than itself. The owl was seeking voles.

When I began to consider the mountain hare I was bewildered by the number of names in use. It is surely time that naturalists decided to use only one of them. It is commonly referred to as blue hare, from the grey-blue film of fine hair on its summer coat, but this name is inappropriate to winter, which is the time of its greatest prominence. The name 'variable hare' may be correct but I consider it ugly. The hare is both attractive and vital, deserving of something better. Alpine hare, white hare, mountain hare are other commonly used names.

MacGillivray, in his natural history of Deeside, used two other local names: changing hare and grey hare. And he mentioned that "of late years it has become much more numerous in Braemar". The hare continually sheds its hair, he added, "except for about four months in winter and spring, so that specimens in good condition for stuffing are not usually to be had. . . . In summer, the head is reddish-brown, the lips and chin brownish-white, the ears dusky, anteriorly edged with red, the upper part of the body dusky-grey, the limbs reddish-grey."

Autumn's animal was "brownish-red, the eyes circled with whitish, the lips light behind; the upper parts of the body reddish-brown, posteriorly tinged with blueish-grey, the forepart of the neck brownish-grey, the limbs yellowish-red. In winter and spring, the fur white, excepting the tips of the ears, which are edged with black at all seasons, and some long hairs scattered over the body. It appears to me that in this species of hare the pile is, like the plumage of the ptarmigan, always changing, not in colour merely but by the substitution of new for old hairs."

I had been told that the pelt of the mountain hare is worthless, and this point was made by MacGillivray, who wrote that "at every season the hairs have so little hold of the skin that they may be pulled out as if from semiputrid skin. . . . In winter, the hair is of an entirely different texture, being much denser, finer and softer, with less gloss, than in autumn."

As if our story has not become complicated enough, there is the additional point that brown and mountain hare may become intermixed and, possibly, they have interbred. Archibald Thorburn, whose paintings of birds in their setting have never lost their power to impress, noticed that "the mountain hare does not always keep to his hilly fastnesses, but will often come down to the lower ground in hard weather, and when it meets the brown hare on the lower levels the two species will interbreed". Modern naturalists are scared off by such simple and bald pronouncements. Interbreeding is possible—but is it common enough to be really significant?

Observant folk of every recent age have been fascinated by the mountain hare in relation to the brown hare. Twice on one day did John Colquhoun, sportsman-writer of the nineteenth century, shoot fine specimens of both. "The difference between them, when thus closely compared, was very perceptive," he asserted. "The head of the alpine was much rounder, which was rendered more obvious by the shortness of its ears. The scut was also ludicrously small; while the roundness of the body was increased by the soft and very thick coat of fur, which made that of the common hare appear hard and wiry. . . . During a mild winter, when the ground is free from snow, the white hare invariably chooses the thickest patch of heather it can find, as if aware of its conspicuous appearance; and to beat all, the bushy tufts on the side and at the foot of rocky hills. . . ."

Because the mountain hare is extraordinarily common on the north-eastern moors, it tends to be the most prominent of the animals that go white—or whitish—in winter. On the road to Tomintoul I disturbed a red grouse and watched the bird skim the heather, building up speed with rapid wingbeats and then gliding and turning to pitch down with becking calls. Here was a bird that had lost the habit of dressing in all-over white. In its hilltop haunts, the ptarmigan makes the transition when winter is approaching—yet the dotterel, that other bird of the hilltops, does not emulate it. The dotterel escapes winter in Scotland by migrating to the shores of the Mediterranean. The snowy owl—

which has been seen on the Cairngorms—is eternally whitish, as befits a bird inhabiting the Arctic. If these owls continue to nest in Britain they will possibly, in due course—say a few thousand years!—learn to moderate their plumage. By that time there could be another Ice Age upon us!

Mountain hares are well named, for they range up the Cairngorms to around four thousand feet and are not generally seen much below fifteen hundred feet, which is the upper limit of the kingdom of the brown hare. Snow is therefore almost certain to lie long in the mountain hare's terrain. There is a gradual transition to white. For a month or two, as daylight hours decline and the temperature falls, the mountain hare replaces its brownish coat, and conversely there is a return to brownish colouration as, with the coming of spring, the days lengthen and the temperature begins to climb again.

Going white in winter must be beneficial in the long term or it would have ceased to occur. If mild winters were the rule, and snow cover was slight, the mountain hare would be at a disadvantage. Predators—including fox, stoat, golden eagle, even buzzard—are everywhere waiting to pounce on the incautious hare.

The mountain hare has learnt subterfuge; it does not flaunt itself during the daytime when conditions are bright. As I saw beside the road to Tomintoul, the hares were emerging from their daytime resting places in the half light. At first glance, a Highland moor is a bleak, bare spot where all the vegetation keeps its head down. Yet hares successfully conceal themselves in heaps of stones or under the cover of heather. When a winter gale hurls snow at the high hills, and then heaps up the snow, hares tend to make for those areas where the wind is strongest and deep drifting is unlikely. In a hollow there is a danger of being overblown. Mountain hares also may snuggle into shallow burrows from which they watch the wind zipping by.

Lea MacNally, presenting an incomparable collection of Scottish wildlife studies in the form of slides when the British Deer Society met for its annual meeting at Perth, showed a picture of a hare lying at the sheltered side of a rock and remaining there until Lea was only twelve feet away. The hare moved, but Lea stood still with all the concentration of a Highland stalker. He watched the hare slowly return to its original position.

When I went to Deeside I was unprepared for the sheer number of mountain hares. Thousands of hares are shot each winter. The flesh is sold locally or despatched to the Continent; the pelts are discarded as being commercially useless. If they could claim high prices there would be some new fortunes to be made in the Highlands.

A Perthshire man described for me an expedition he had made to the Ochils. Twenty-two guns were stationed on high ground and beaters moved along the foothills, flushing the hares, which tended to climb—into a shower of pellets from the guns. During three day's shooting over two thousand hares were slain.

I queried the effect of such mass slaughter on the hare population. The man said, "Mountain hares take a turn at dying out; then they come back again. We can go on to the hill —as we did three weeks ago—and shoot one thousand hares in a week. For a time we might not see a hare in that stretch of country. Another year the district will be alive with hares again." Generally speaking, it is a natural cycle—the sort that affects most animal communities.

You may recall that I met a stalker by the Cairnwell Pass who had intended to go on a hare shoot. The event was cancelled. He told me, "If that shoot had been held, we would probably have killed about five hundred hares." And I used to think that the mountain hare was uncommon! It is certainly less common than it was in the north-west of Scotland, but the moors around Deeside seemed to heave with hares at the time of my visit.

The stalker volunteered the information that mountain hare are more communally-minded in winter than at other times. They may stay in 'batches', usually near flattish ground, where the sweetest herbage grows. Feeding occurs at dawn and dusk—

probably also through the night. Of the many hares forced from the high ground in bad weather, the stalker said, only the good hares returned to the tops. The others were apt to stay on the lower ground where he called them "bog hares".

Winter is still in command of the landscape when the first stirrings of the breeding urge are detectable, though in some snow-blasted years breeding will be delayed. A profusion of hares demands a high breeding rate, and the hare is excessively productive. Litters are found mainly from about March through to August. A doe might have two or three litters a year, and the stalker said that on average there were two young to a litter. In his experience, three leverets in a family was not common. "They're dropped among the heather; then the doe moves them about. If one leveret is found—maybe by a fox—the others might escape."

The hare I viewed at last light went out of sight, over the crest of a near horizon. Twenty-five yards further on, I stopped to inspect another hare, and then there was a squashed corpse to be examined. This hare had perished under the wheels of a car.

Further along the road I saw that the land sloped away, levelled out and then rose again to a high hill. In this large moorland arena I could locate the forms of mountain hares with childish ease, even with the naked eye. Some hares crouched as they fed. Others, standing on their hind legs and quarters, peered far over the heather as though they were afraid of missing something. Three hares stood close together, and two others indulged in a mild bout of boxing.

The short-eared owl reappeared and patrolled the moor. Three times did it make a sudden quarter turn and plunge to the ground in its quest for short-tailed voles. Another owl of the same species regarded me gravely from its perch on a tree as I returned to Deeside. A roe deer stood in a patch of birch and looked as insubstantial as a shadow.

Mountain hares had now gone out of my mind, for ahead I saw the dark hulk and the snowy pinnacles of Lochnagar. There were, I had heard, whole battalions of mountain hares on Lochnagar—also ptarmigan that now were in winter white. When these creatures were casting the white fur and feathers, the golden plover would be back on Lochnagar. And the dunlin would be trilling, its call light as gossamer.

12

WRECK OF CALEDON

Think of Deeside and it does not take much mental effort to recall the hills. They almost seal off the upper valley from the rest of Scotland. These big, brown, heather-and-peat lumps and blue-grey turrets of rock are especially memorable when iced over like wedding cakes after winter storms. The hills give Deeside an air of seclusion—of mystery indeed. I think of the topmost reaches, most fondly, as an archetype of the Lost World.

Running the hills a close second in the list of imposing features are the big, dark, mannish fir woods. Hills and woods are complementary, as Coleridge was aware when he wrote:

> And here were forests ancient as the hills,
> Enfolding sunny spots of greenery.

Coleridge may not have been thinking of Deeside, but the words apply. William Smith, stout Victorian, pointed out that the scenic effectiveness of these woodlands lies mostly in their mass and density, "for as a rule they are simply pine woods, larches and spruces commonly with firs".

One can become so sentimental about these northern pinewoods that it leads to an incurable disease. Might it be called Caledonitis? In a strange sort of way, the sufferers do not wish to be cured! Many writers have described the Caledonian Forest as it was before man appeared as though it was some northern

(top) Highland stags and hinds that have converged for feeding
(bottom) Stags near Derry Lodge on the extensive lands of Mar

Highland red stag recovering after being tranquilised

Garden of Eden. Seeing the old 'firs' of upper Deeside, with their twisted roots extending into a porous ground on which ling and blaeberry are plentifully distributed, a discerning visitor tries to picture the area as it was before man began to throw his weight about in the Highland glens.

The Caledonian Forest has been the subject of much scientific research, and figures and facts have been neatly tabulated on reams of foolscap paper, but man still becomes lyrical at the thought of it. A Scotsman of sensitivity thinks of the Caledonian Forest with the sort of lyricism an Englishman reserves for Sherwood Forest or the New Forest. Strangely, the Scottish forest has not thrown up a folk hero like Robin of Sherwood. The Wolf of Badenoch and his attendant thugs came into the Scottish story, but mainly as destroyers.

The harmless exercise of pondering on the story of the Wood of Caledon, as the forest has also been called, usually ends with frustration. The modern mind is so accustomed to a neat and tidy countryside it cannot easily comprehend something that is totally natural—untouched by human hands. Even those remnants of the old forest which are cherished today have had the hand of man upon them.

The Wood of Caledon lay in the main glens and tributary valleys, also running up the hill slopes to a level now attained only by a few stunted and particularly stubborn trees. It became more and more an upland forest. Deeside has a remarkably large remnant of the forest in stern Ballochbuie.

Romantics think nostalgically of the time when everything in the forest was in perfect natural balance. Every day was a sunny day. There was a balance of sorts, but life in the forest was not static. And even where the condition of a climax forest was attained it was less rich in wildlife than many suppose. A forest was subject to many strains and stresses, leading to constant shifts of dominance among various tree species. Long-term changes in the climate resulted in other changes.

Picture, first of all, the conditions that applied before the Wood of Caledon was established. For a vast number of years—

H

and I resist the temptation to document the story neatly with reference to estimates of the precise numbers of years—the dominant feature of the northern landscape was ice, under which nothing could live. The ice sheet overtopped all but the highest hills. Glaciers broadened, deepened and smoothed with soft debris the old river valleys. The ice sheet would retreat at as little as fifty yards a year.

For thousands more years the conditions were sub-Arctic. There was desolation, with unstable rocks and frozen ground, but as warmer conditions prevailed a vegetation of sorts spread out. It was the type now found as arctic alpine islets on high hills such as the Cairngorms. Dotting the primeval landscape would be a few dwarf trees, willows and birches and creatures we could identify, among them the ptarmigan, and snowy owl. Snow buntings would twitter while crossing the scene. This species is now, in Scotland, at the southern edge of its immense breeding range.

The trees advanced broadly from the south. Britain, it should be remembered, was then attached to the Continent. Birch appeared at the edge of the tundra. It was to be known by the Gaelic name of *beith*. This hardy but short-lived pioneer spreads quickly. On the heels of the birch came the Scots pine (in Gaelic, *guis* or *guithais*) which superseded the birch in many areas but did not entirely displace it. The birch remains a common Highland tree and is found farther to the north, and higher up the hills, than any other species.

Pinewood, established from winged seeds strewn by the wind, blotted out considerable tracts. If it had been possible to take a slow-motion film with, say, one frame a year, and then to run the film at normal speed, it would be seen that even an apparently venerable pinewood is not static. We judge it by our life span, which is only a wink when measured against time.

Pines spread up the hills, each tree questing for light. Older parts of the wood would decline through age or natural catastrophe and trees would seed their way back into the voids, meeting up with young pines that were springing from the debris of the fallen or fire-gutted giants. The pine did not have a monopoly in the Wood of Caledon. Other species proved even more successful on certain types of ground, oak, alder, ash, hazel finding their special niches.

Nairn, writing about Highland woods in 1890, gave the range of the Caledonian Forest as "from Glen Lyon and Rannoch to Strathspey and Strathglass, and from Glencoe eastwards to the Braes of Mar". But there was no precise boundary; it was not as firmly fixed in its range as a modern plantation around which fencing is raised. In its long history, the pine forest gained or lost ground according to circumstances. When fire broke out— caused, perhaps, by a flash of lightning during a summer storm —there would be acres of blackened ground and, for a time, a chance for the birch to reassert itself. Gales toppled the young or creakily old trees. Here and there man digs up traces of former forest that died out when, in wet periods, peat developed and clogged the trees.

On many Highland dawns unseen by man the sun quested between the trees and picked out the birds and beasts whose descendants still cling tenaciously to their old heritage: birds like the crested tit, crossbill, capercaillie, osprey; beasts including the red and roe deer, red squirrel, pine marten and wild cat. The first men to reach this area were almost certainly too late to meet the giant Irish elk, in which the evolutionary process had led to grotesquely-enlarged antlers, the combined weight of a pair being up to ninety pounds. The finest skeletons have been found in Hibernian bogs, but the Irish elk was more widely distributed. Its finest days were when it grazed open country before the trees spread. It was already doomed as a species when man was struggling to assert himself much farther south.

Again in fairly open areas, especially where standing water had coppices of willow around it, the elk that was the Old World version of the North American moose emerged to stand in the shallows and feed. This elk sustained its enormous bulk by stuffing itself with water lilies and other soggy vegetation.

The northern lynx and the reindeer joined the list of vanished species when man appeared. Man hunted to oblivion the beavers that had champed their industrious way through small trees and dragged the trunks over land and through water for the reinforcement of dams and lodges. The last of the brown bears was persecuted to its death by man about ten centuries ago. In due course the wolf and wild boar were to be only the stuff of memories.

Much wildlife remains. The fluty whistle of the otter might be heard, as it was in antiquity. Man can still sit near a sett in the woods and, after an hour or so, be rewarded by the sight of a black-and-white striped head at the entrance, marking the emergence of a badger, which is bear-like in some of its ways. Brock sometimes shuffles about the woods in winter, but May is the best time for badger-watching. Then a sow is seen to lead out its cubs, which call loudly in play. There is entertainment value in the sight of a badger carrying fresh bedding into the sett. It clasps the bedding between forelegs and lower jaw and shuffles backwards into its subterranean quarters.

The deer remain, with the red deer in the marginal areas and the roe, generally speaking, true forest dwellers—and very parochial. Roe deer do not like to be crowded and so conditions in the wideflung Caledonian Forest suited these animals, also the red squirrel. The modern mind would boggle at the former numbers and variety of birds of prey—golden and white-tailed eagles, goshawks and kites.

A forest of the Caledonian type was not peculiar to Scotland. There were so-called Scots pines all the way from Spain to Russia. In some of the Continental forests one might still savour the old atmosphere.

I have visited most of the Scottish relict pinewoods. The oldest trees I saw were perhaps three hundred years of age, which means they had grown since man began his commercial onslaught on the forest. The giants, in girth as well as height, tend to be those gawky, mis-shapen specimens that escaped the axe because they were of little value. Now they have character. Modern plantations tend to be depressing places. The young conifers are set out in ranks, and most of them are 'exotics'—introduced species, of which two examples from North America are the sitka spruce (by far the most popular species for planting) and the lodgepole pine, which was used by Red Indians when making wigwams!

A pinewood with some claim to be natural contains pines of uneven ages. The veterans wear their bark like reptilian scales, and the upper bark has usually peeled, glowing with an orangy-red that looks superb in evening sunlight. Pines do not naturally crowd each other, and so there is built up on the ground a vegetation of surprising richness—heathy plants like *Calluna* and *Erica*, fruiting plants like blaeberry and cowberry, and diminutive plants of which the chickweed wintergreen is a good example.

It is only in recent years that we have realised that the earth's resources are limited—and, indeed, that we are using them up at great speed. Early man, still overawed by his surroundings, doubtless thought that the woods were inexhaustible. He was wrong. The best and most easily worked land was that to the south of the Highland Line, and it had lost its magnificent tree cover by the twelfth century as agriculture took over. North of the Highland Line, burning a stretch of forest was the most efficient way of flushing out enemies—men or wolves. But farming called the tune. Ever more land was cleared for man's domestic stock and crops. Highland families who moved to the high hills in summer with their cattle and a few sheep caused further denudation.

The large Deeside and Speyside forests were saved for a time by their remoteness and the difficulty of extracting the timber. Political squabbles also arrested the 'development'. When tempers had calmed after the Jacobite rebellion, big business was quick to move in. An ingenious way of abstracting timber was found, the trunks of the pines felled in the wilds being lashed together in the form of rafts and sent down the rivers to the sea, where industries developed to handle them. It was a careless age, marked by felling but little planting. Wasteful forest fires began accidentally. The resinous timber spluttered and crackled as a fire rampaged for a week or more before dousing itself at the river.

Fortunately there were men in the eighteenth and nineteenth centuries who replenished the timber resources through ambitious planting schemes. Sir Walter Scott, in his *Heart of Midlothian* (1818) had the dying laird of Dumbie-dykes advising Jack, his son, with the words: "Ye may be aye sticking in a tree. It will be growing, while ye're sleeping." Big landowners did more than stick in the odd tree. Many glens were given a substantial coverlet of timber.

The slow evolutionary processes will not do for modern man. He plants, fertilises, thins and clear-fells in the space of a few decades. None of his commercial conifers, it seems, will have the chance to attain that old age in which a tree becomes characterful. I have heard talk of pulp mills being built at the centre of conifered areas, the trees being regarded as so much vegetable fibre to be pushed into the maw of the mill.

The good forester has a soul. He is not so obsessed by growing trees that he cannot provide for some of the wild creatures that gather in the forests. Visitors to some Forestry Commision holdings are encouraged to follow nature trails (booklets in hand) and to enjoy the wealth of birds, animals and plants.

The modern naturalist envies Sir Robert Gordon, who wrote in the seventeenth century about the "vert and venaison" of the county of Sutherland. It should be remembered, however, that the creatures mentioned were not necessarily of woodland. Sir Robert's Sutherland had not been renowned for timber. He announced that "all these forests and chases are very profitable for feeding for bestiall and delectable for hunting," being "full of reid deer, roes, woulffs, foxes, wyld catts, brocks, skuyrells, whittrets, weasels, otters, martrixes, hares and foumarts. In These fforests, and in all this province, ther is great store of partridges, pluviers, capercaleys, black coaks, mure fowls, hethhens, swanes, bewters, turtle-doves, herons, dowes, steares or starlings, lairigig, or knag (which is a fowl like unto a parokeet or parrot, which makes place for nest with her beek in the oak-tree), duke, draig, widgeon, teale, wild-goose, ringoose, gouls, wharps, shot wharps, woodcocks, larkes, sparrows, snyps, black-buirds, and all other kinds of wild-fowl, and birds which are to be had in any part of this kingdom." Many of them found places in the Wood of Caledon.

If, as some suspect, we are living in an interglacial period, then one day the ice will return and slowly sweep away all in its path. For tens of thousands of years the ice sheet will lie thickly on the landscape. Then will begin a steady retreat, and a return to the old sequence of tundra, birch and pine.

I hope that people at some future time will be more kindly disposed towards the Second Wood of Caledon.

13

QUEEN'S PINEWOOD

Ballochbuie is a delightful name for the largest area of ancient pinewood in Scotland. Its trees stand darkly along the banks of the Dee, 950 feet above sea level. The wood extends up steep slopes and peters out where timber reaches the limit of its endurance and coarse grasses take over. Ballochbuie is on the royal estate, Balmoral, but when the Queen is not in residence some of the tracks may be used by strangers. Well-beaten routes zig-zag through the forest towards the snowy bastions of Lochnagar.

Queen Victoria saved Ballochbuie when it was threatened by forestry interests. Instead of being clear-felled the wood has been left in a reasonably natural state; parts of it, indeed, have been fenced off to give the pine seedlings a chance to grow, which they would not have in the normal way through the browsing of the deer.

Ballochbuie bears the marks of the self-regenerating forest. The trees are of various ages, not packed in limited space and uniform of size, as they are in most commercial forests. King of Ballochbuie is the Scots pine, with juniper forming a generous attendant layer in some areas.

Among the pines and junipers for many years have flitted roe and red deer. Scrope, writing in 1839, commented on the abundance of roe. He also stated that the red deer "are frequently, more especially in cold or windy weather, to be seen within shot of the drives: and both stags and hinds have often been killed by Mr Farquharson from a carriage or a pony. The deer are seldom driven, and never hunted with dogs, unless to bring down a wounded animal."

Balmoral Castle was still five miles distant when, having set off from Braemar, I saw the pines of Ballochbuie. They clustered beyond a river that was still young and forceful, as yet not having developed a middle-aged spread. Some hills looked so close I felt I could reach out and put my cap on the summits.

The Farquharsons bought Ballochbuie from McGregor, last laird of the area, the bargain being sealed with the gift of a tartan. Queen Victoria bought the wood for a reputed £100,000 in 1878 and, typically, had a large memorial stone erected, Ballochbuie was described as "the bonniest plaid in Scotland", alluding to the tartan exchanged between the McGregors and the Farquharsons. The wood was virtually left alone—though when Edward VII inherited the estate he had some pine felled and sawn up to provide new panelling for the hall at Balmoral Castle, replacing some panelling he considered to be drab.

I stood beside the main valley road and scrutinised the dark, drool pines right up to the point at which I could also see the snowfields of Lochnagar. Every dark dot in the sky was examined in case it was a golden eagle. Pairs of eagles nest in pines in the higher parts of the forest. Then I let my gaze fall again to Ballochbuie, of which Sir T. D. Lauder might have been thinking when he described pines that "run up all the ramifications and subdivisions of the tributary valleys, cover the lower elevations, climb the sides of the higher hills, and even in many cases approach the very roots of the giant mountains which tower over them".

It is almost a century since the Farquharsons' hold on Ballochbuie was relinquished. Their old mansion, Invercauld House, remains in their hands. Its façade may be clearly seen by those travelling down the valley from Braemar. The house was enlarged and partly rebuilt a year or two before Queen Victoria collected the title deeds of Ballochbuie. Did the purchase price of the forest help them with their special building expenses? The building features a 70-feet-high castellated tower.

The Farquharsons were long established in Deeside when Pennant passed by in 1769, noticing that "the whole tract abounds with game; the stags at this time were ranging in the mountains, but the little roebucks were perpetually bounding before us; and the black game often sprung from under our feet".

Before halting at the edge of Ballochbuie, I had motored over a bridge built at the expense of Prince Albert. He also improved the highway running north of the river, so that today one travels on long straight stretches. Albert was not being benevolent for the sake of benevolence—though he was, generally, a warm-hearted man. He wanted to preserve the privacy of Balmoral estate (to the south of the river) by closing the old road there. The closure was brought about by an Act of Parliament in 1855. Six miles were erased from the public road network of the Highlands.

More than that, the old Bridge o' Dee was closed to traffic (which was why the new bridge had been built) and today it stands in a grand isolation, "like a well bent bow", one of the most attractive bridges in the country. Its builders did not have beauty in mind. They were constructing a military road from Perth to Inverness in 1753 and the river Dee must be crossed. The bridge was part of a road scheme whereby the Highlanders were pacified after the Jacobite troubles.

Every traveller must have noticed Craig Clunie, an almost perpendicular rock that totally dominates the present main road, casting a deep shadow across it. Trees growing on Craig Clunie must be among the most daring in Britain. Soldiers were hardly likely to go scrambling six hundred feet above road level on slopes where even a goat would feel dizzy, and during the stormy days of 1715 the Farquharsons stored the charters of their estate in a small cave there.

I rested my elbows on a parapet of the bridge and watched an angler stride from the shallows of the river. He went through the protracted process of packing away his rod and tackle, The angler had been trying for salmon, using an artificial fly named 'Jenny'. This, and one called 'Logie', were the most devastating items in his armoury, but there were others—'Blue Charm', 'Silver Blue' and 'Sweep'.

Fly-fishing for salmon is a refined art favouring the salmon, but the local people were once brutally disposed towards the fish. Queen Victoria watched a hundred or more of her tenants paddling in the river, prodding and moving stones, trying to net the bewildered salmon. Men carried fish spears, leisters, known more specifically by the number of prongs they bore—taw, three or fower. The odds against a salmon passing through were lengthening when a fishing act of 1868 prohibited leistering.

A few years later concern at the dwindling stocks of salmon was being expressed by the Dee Salmon Fishing Improvement. Not only were the river people being unsporting, but salmon found it hard to escape from the many nets arranged at the coast. Russel, writing in 1864, noted that "a sail along almost any portion of the coast of Scotland . . . will show that the shore is draped with salmon nets, with very little regard to the neighbourhood or distance of a river".

There is romance for me in considering or observing the spawning run of salmon. These fish cross the North Atlantic from plankton-rich waters under the polar ice cap where they have grown enormously. Some of them are nosing their way into the Dee in November, which is the time of the main run. The most satisfying time for fishing the upper reaches is from the middle of May until the last week in June, and salmon are showing their fins in the shallows of the topmost stretches in July or August. Spawning takes place on the gravel beds in September and October.

I was told that the average Dee salmon weighs from eight pounds to ten pounds, but naturally fish of greater weight have been landed, one of them making the scales dip at thirty pounds. Sea trout run up the Dee in July. The run once ended at about

Aboyne, but the angler told me with delight that trout are now venturing farther up the river.

Walking into Ballochbuie I thought of William MacGillivray, whose impressive book on the natural history of Deeside was published in 1855, being privately circulated by command of the Queen. MacGillivray was a man of humble origins. He did not become arrogant or over-assertive on his rise to prominence. He was an islander, from the far west of Scotland, who studied at Aberdeen and during vacations strode home and back to university across the whole breadth of Scotland. So he came to know Deeside in the finest way—on foot, travelling at about three miles an hour.

Sir Arther Tansley strode in Ballochbuie when he gathered information for his work on natural plant associations. Byron, who spent his youth at Aberdeen and visited the Ballater district on holiday, reached Ballochbuie in the company of a ghillie in 1803. The two climbed Lochnagar. Byron, according to the ghillie, sat meditatively at the edge of the cliffs.

Ballochbuie is not all ancient pine. I passed young timber, which had little more than the girth of pit props, and noticed men engaged in drainage work, their spades cutting through spongy peat as they lowered the water table to encourage deeper rooting. Near them was a curious-looking vehicle, a Unimog.

A gate led through a sawmill-fresh deer fence whose timber was almost white. It would appear skeletal at dusk. The saws at the mill had unlocked an age-old scent, the fence having a delicious resinous tang. Some titmice scolded me, but generally bird life was sparse. At times, with the air still and little to see beyond trees and vegetation, I felt conspicuously alone.

Crossbills nest in Ballochbuie. These are birds of the old native stock, not the Continental cousins which, from time to time, erupt in vast numbers from the endless forests of northern Europe, some to have a British landfall. The cock crossbill wears a scarlet coat, its mate being attired in green. Both have twisted mandibles which are used to screw off the scales of cones, exposing the nourishing seeds, their main items of food. Incidentally, when crossbills arrived in 1810, the *Aberdeen Journal* wrote of the "Crossbill, or German parrot".

My last view of Highland crossbills had been near Loch Garten, in Speyside. I heard a crackling sound, like cones expanding in the heat—for the day was sunny and hot. Then, faintly in the still air, came the sound made as pieces of cone slithered to the ground over the tree's bunched needles. The crossbills were feeding fifteen feet away from where I stood. Not until I had worked my way around the thirty foot tree, and stared and squinted alternatively in the patches of sunlight, did I clearly see the birds.

Crested tits have been spreading from the ancestral haunts on Speyside. A short time before I watched my crossbills near Loch Garten one of the young volunteer watchers near the osprey nest put some slivers of cheese on a bird table and attracted a crested tit.

Now, in my Ballochbuie walk, I was heading for those areas of the forest that Captain Blair Oliphant had in mind when he contributed to a book dealing with the sporting qualities of Edward VII and noted that on Ballochbuie's exposed slopes "the trees are stunted and irregular, and here and there a bare scarp of rock shows between. Beneath is an undergrowth of misty-green juniper and heather, with a carpet of deep mosses and blaeberries half hiding the great grey boulders that are scattered over it".

In one of the high parts of the forest, three capercaillie cocks left a senile pine and went rattling off. It would have been virtually impossible to detect the birds in advance. My footfalls had, however, been muffled by dead needles on the path. I could surely have got a little nearer before the birds left.

Capercaillie do not flock as such, and there are usually two or three birds in a wintering group. Each bird stuffs coarse pine needles into its crop, where the grit it has eaten helps with the breakdown of the tough fare. A wintering capercaillie eats voraciously but does not derive very much nourishment from the pine needles, as I have observed. There is a steady loss of weight until the food bounty that comes with spring.

The capercaillie is tolerated—up to a point—by the forester who suffers most from its depredations. Now and again a hunt is organised by landowners who have the capercaillie driven to the gun. The flesh of the bird is eaten without real pleasure, having a strong piny flavour.

For a capercaillie the pine needle may be dull and tough but at least there are plenty of needles to eat. Many creatures have a hard time when snow falls, sealing off the ground. Snow quickly tumbles from the pine branches and, while eating, the capercaillie can select sheltered areas where the winter blast has been reduced by the outlying trees to a gentle breeze.

The capercaillie were descendants of Swedish birds brought to Scotland by Lord Breadalbane of Taymouth Castle. The native stock had been exterminated, and when the Game Act of 1831 passed through Parliament the capercaillie was not mentioned; there were no birds to take into account. The drier, eastern side of Scotland is more favourable to the bird than the damper west, and in the east I have had some memorable views of this largest grouse in the world.

A cyclist on Balmoral Estate had possibly the finest views of all as he drove through an area where a cock bird, full of breeding fervour, and rather pugnacious, attacked him and tried to knock him from his machine, which had violated the bird's territory!

George Logan tells me that it is possible to sooth a caper by music. He parked his vehicle during a mid-day break while working in a pinewood and, switching on the radio, listened to the strains of classical music. A cock caper approached, stopped and moved its head from side to side as though in appreciation of the music. The head movements stopped when George switched to another radio station and jazz (then a current craze) blared out through the wood. When a return was made to the radio station providing classical music, the caper advanced almost to the door of the car. (The effect of jazz on a roe doe was to make the animal advance to the car and stand with ripples of excitement running along its spine!)

Several times during his Highland career in forestry, George Logan drove along a track in a 'black wood' and, seeing a hen caper leading a brood from one side to the other, stopped his vehicle, clambered out and, for amusement, lifted up the last of the brood. "As soon as the hen bird became aware of this, it became fierce," said George. "If, as sometimes happened, there was a cock caper not far away, I dropped the chick and retreated!"

Late one evening in May I saw a caper cock in all its splendour while motoring along a road between birch woods. A dark head only could be seen to the right of the road, from which the ground sloped downwards. The rest of the bird was concealed in a dip. The caper emerged and stood on the road. I stopped my car a little way beyond the majestic creature, which strode slowly, haughtily across the highway.

Another car approached, and the driver, seeing the caper, stopped to let it pass. There was a gap of maybe twenty yards between the two vehicles and the caper, continuing its walk without pausing, passed through this space. The other driver must not have been a naturalist, for he immediately moved off. Did he think that the caper was a feral turkey? Reversing my own car as the caper moved into a tangle of coarse vegetation I saw this twelve pound bird standing only fifteen feet from the roadway.

Earlier, in the distance, the capercaillie looked black, but now it was seen to be a very dark grey, the feathers sheened with green. There was brown on the wings. The head, small for the size of the bird, was topped off by scarlet wattles. The caper waddled towards a fence of wire mesh, which it cleared with a vigorous leap and a flap. Then it strode deeper into the wood, stopping to survey my car derisively.

Mounting excitement destroyed its pose. The big bird became airborne, on whirring wings that at first were flapped desperately, as though the bird was not quite sure of their adequacy. The caper flew, levelled out at about twenty feet and glided for a while.

There were two lingering impressions. Once the flurry of take-off was over the bird made little sound, and although it might appear to be large and clumsy it had a light touch when navigating between the trunks of many varied trees. Caper, indeed, wing their way round the trunks and big branches but tend to crash through small stuff!

Another capercaillie crashed to a halt on a silver birch across the road. It was a hen bird, though indistinct because in viewing it I also looked into the lightest part of the sky, losing much of the fine detail. Perched on an upthrusting branch about 35 feet from the ground, the caper stood perfectly balanced, adequately braced, with one leg at a higher position than the other. This caper left the area noisily but returned to pitch down on a birch standing on the other side of the road. It was from this perch that it watched me drive away. The range was only twenty yards.

Ballochbuie had been recommended to me as a place for capercaillie. My informant did not mention deer, but here the roe have adequate cover and food and the red deer are specially favoured. They are woodland deer as opposed to the stock which must survive on the open hill. The wood offers shelter and good browse.

I had little shelter when I broke out of tree cover at a high level and heard the wind moaning around crags. Snow was falling in thick wraiths. Looking down, where Ballochbuie had a tangle of undergrowth and comparatively few trees, I saw a hind calf, then a hind standing in partial cover a few yards away. The hind stalked away, and its excited offspring bounced just behind it down the slope.

The two deer lost themselves in Ballochbuie with infuriating ease—and hardly any sound after the initial crackling of vegetation as they sped away. They gave the impression of heading for the other side of the parish but might even then be circling, eventually to stand head-on to me in the gloom, where

Mar stags converging on a feeding ground

Mounted heads of red deer shot on the hills around Deeside

(*top*) The Bridge of Dee, once part of a military way (*bottom*) Near the head of Glen Muick

they would be undetectable. Peter Delap refers to the "lace curtain dilemma", when the deer being sought is under cover and in shade. It peers in comfort and security—like an old lady from behind lace curtains—at the man who moves before it in bright light.

The path broke out of the forest where the trees were standing in bunches rather than as a continuous mass. The wind seemed to have that little extra in chilling qualities, cooled by sweeping the snowfields. My face was so cold as I stood in the wind that when flakes of snow alighted I was aware only of their wetness.

My return to the road was undertaken at a jaunty pace, with a pause near where a waterfall roared out like a prophet in the wilderness. I saw the nests of black ants. Fallen branches had been debarked by woodland creatures which might have chewed the bark, working it like gobbets of chewing gum. Or did they simply want to reach the sappy area underneath? In the half light the debarked pieces would have a luminous quality.

I was trudging at a steady three miles an hour when I saw the next group of deer—two hinds and a calf of the year startled, by my sudden and speedy appearance, into movement through the young plantation I had seen when first entering Ballochbuie. The calf was sturdy now. It would complete its first year in about the following June and then become a jennack.

I had not seen stags because, at that moment, there was a great gathering of them outside the keeper's house. Over 180 deer milled about on a broad sweep of grassland which looked like an arena because ranks of Scots pines and other conifers were grouped around. With the stags, though keeping at the periphery of the throng, were two hinds and two calves.

The females were timid, which could not be said for the stags, now thoroughly accustomed to the feeding routine. They were not exactly thrustful but their manner reflected impatience. There was much snorting and some sparring as animals met

I

antler to antler. The cold wind swirled as though it had lost its way between the pines.

The keeper lifted hay, turnips, nuts and potatoes on to a Land-Rover, which was driven by his wife during the distribution of food. I saw the provisions being tossed out as the vehicle covered the ground in an orderly fashion. Then a mass of blocky, brown-grey bodies, and a mini-forest of antlers, obscured it. One of the Queen's stags was a thirteen-pointer, the much-vaunted Imperial.

The deer had come to lower ground in November, and after wintering in sheltered areas many of the stags would cast their antlers here before returning to the hill for the summer.

The weather could still provide some surprises. In the year before my visit snow fell on the high hills in June!

14

A SQUIRREL'S WORLD

Ballochbuie—and other large 'black woods' in the Highlands—can have about them that calm one associates with big churches. Tread on a twig, and the crack seems to reverberate for seconds on end. I fancy that every creature within a mile has flicked up its ears and waits for the next explosive sound. An excited titmouse churs with the noise intensity of a pneumatic drill. Goldcrest talk, normally a faint whisper, seems to clatter like sewing machines.

On such a day it is pointless to look for roe or red deer. Their early warning devices—in particular, their hearing and scenting—pick up intrusion far enough away for the deer to be able to keep permanently out of sight. Do not presume that if you do not see a deer the area is deerless. The gruff bark of a departing roe signifies that the animal is aware of being detected. But how many roe have slunk silently away up to that point?

There have been many still and quiet days in the long story of the Caledonian Forest, especially those parts of it that were climax woods, mature and self-assured. If a visitor's interest lies in ticking off bird and animal species as he sees them, he will be disappointed in the old pinewood. At the best of times the wild creatures are thinly distributed. Wildlife can be quite scarce in winter.

On really quiet days I listen for the red squirrel, which thankfully is still numbered among the occupants of the Highland pinewoods, including Ballochbuie. Squirrels play hide and seek with an intruder, a pursuit that stands the best chance of success in the early morning or late evening.

Go to Ballochbuie on a day when you might almost hear a pine needle drop and you should detect the rasping sound as a squirrel dashes up the fissured bark of a pine. There will be another—much louder—type of rasping when the animal chatters. With height attained, the squirrel looks down from a substantial branch that partly obscures it from anyone on the ground. If really annoyed it stamps its forefeet, twitches its tail and loudly swears!

There is a friendliness about the Highland red squirrel at most times. One inevitably recalls tales that Miss Potter told about Squirrel Nutkin. Who can think of the squirrel as a rodent when it is seen feasting, swirling the food with its forepaws as its chisel teeth work it over, like sharp-edged tools touching a lathe? Or when just the squirrel's head and soft eyes are visible as it peers around a tree? Or, as I have seen at the edge of Rothiemurchus in Speyside, an animal frolics on the fence of the guest house and then takes a turn at acrobatics on the clothes line?

Squirrel-watching is a delight for all times of the year—except, perhaps, in wild winter weather, when the squirrel stays in cover. It does not hibernate in the true sense. There is no autumnal stuffing-in of food to be followed by many weeks of torpidity. On crisp winter days the squirrel flaunts itself and its movement on a pine tree sends cascades of fine snow pouring to the ground.

What the squirrel, and other forest creatures, do not care for is that sort of wet and blustery weather that draggles their hair. Or high winds which make the more elderly pines wheeze asthmatically. Then the sounds of approaching danger are hard to detect and the animals are generally jittery.

During a second Ballochbuie expedition I came under the calm stare of a squirrel—a stare which, so the experts deduce, is monochromatic. My squirrel had been exploring the ground litter. It bounded towards the nearest tree with a series of graceful movements during which its tail was kept clear of the ground.

If the squirrel had remained on the ground I could possibly have outpaced it, but the claws of the animal touched the trunk of a pine and the progress of the squirrel vertically was so swift it almost took *my* breath away. Highland squirrels needed special agility in the old forest days when they had a natural predator in the pine marten. It scampered about the trees with equal verve.

The squirrel I watched stopped now and again to assure itself I was still present and had not moved. Little more than the head was visible as it craned around the tree to fix its black eyes on me. In view, a little later, was more of the creature; it lacked the bright redness of the summer, for since the moult its coat had become a rather dull brownish-grey. The squirrel used an escape route that was in part a footway, along the pine branches, in part an airway, for if there was a wide gap between branches the animal confidently leapt into space.

Deeside has a modest stock of red squirrels at a time when much of Britain is infested with grey squirrels, whose ancestors were natives of North America. They were brought to this country to enhance—it was thought—the local fauna. In many areas the grey put in a successful take-over bid for the woods. It thrives despite campaigns against it, partly because it has become the darling of suburban housewives. A Perthshire gamekeeper mentioned to me, quietly, rather hesitantly, as though it was something of which to be ashamed, that the grey squirrel had been seen in his district.

The grey squirrel looks attractive—until you watch the red squirrel, which is smaller, daintier, altogether more colourful—and native British! (We will forget, for the moment, that when the Highland stock was almost extinct towards the end of the eighteenth century the Duke of Atholl brought in some red squirrels from Scandinavia to repopulate the woods at Dunkeld, and the species spread again).

The Highland red squirrel of the Caledonian Forest lived a quiet life. It had few competitors and abundant food. There was no necessity for it to become one of a crowd. The red squirrel still prefers to be a loner, when it is not engaged in rearing a family. It also reacts poorly to significant changes in its habitat.

When extensive timber felling took place during the eighteenth century the red squirrel was brought to the edge of extinction, whereas the more adaptable pine marten took to the hills, living among the rocks, eventually to return to woodland through large-scale modern afforestation. One of the important refuges of the red squirrel down the years has been Rothiemurchus, the big pinewood in Speyside.

The world is never constant. There are boom years and years of scarcity. The weather has its ups and downs. Scots pines have years of bounty and years when the trees produce few cones. Monica Shorten, who has studied red squirrels intently, believes that the squirrel population has an eight year cycle. During that time boom is followed by crash and recovery. 'Stress' factors are involved in the population crash.

To the red squirrel, pine seeds are vital in winter, when its diet includes little more than this monotonous fare. The animal's food is broader-based in summer, taking in buds and bulbs. Squirrels undoubtedly damage trees. They do not usually pass a bird's nest without inquiring into its contents, which are then likely to be consumed. I shudder to think how many Scottish crossbills, which have similar haunts and main food preferences to the red squirrel, are destroyed by an animal that can so easily reach their nests. The crested tit is another sufferer.

The squirrel is now relatively immune from predators and is no longer slaughtered by all and sundry. In its northern forests it copes with the rearing of one family a year. Squirrels in the South of England can usually manage two families. The enemies of a red squirrel would appear to be other red squirrels, an abundance leading to population troubles, and the ever-changing world in which their preferred habitat is constantly threatened.

I have never seen a free-ranging pine marten, which made its stand on the hills of north-west Scotland but is now, happily, spreading out again. One or two have been sighted to the south of the Great Glen. The marten, like the squirrel, has an appreciable plumed tail, in its case one about a foot long. In winter the marten assumes a coat of rich chocolate-brown, with a creamy throat patch. A shy creature, it mainly moves at night. Once it was heavily persecuted for its pelt.

The marten steadily gains ground under cover of the big new plantations. The Scottish squirrel, which recovered its numbers with the help of introductions from overseas, clings tenaciously to its ancient heritage. Ballochbuie squirrels seem to go about their lives with a tolerance of man, especially if he is not too inquisitive or assertive. If you see a squirrel, stand still for a while. Let the animal become accustomed to you. It will not be long before it regards you as an innocuous part of the scene.

15

ROYAL JAUNTS

Did Balmoral exist? Or was it just a mirage among the dark fir woods between Braemar and Ballater? With its 100-feet-high tower of gleaming Abergeldie granite, the castle seemed to float like a white ship on a dark sea. Because Balmoral had been effectively screened by tree and high fence, views of the castle from the public road were momentary. It needed a real effort of concentration—or a picture in a guide book—for me to recall its precise form. Almost all the Balmoral estate lies to the south of the Dee, the only incursion north being a bridgehead in a literal sense—the Bridge of Dee—on which I had already stood, though the Queen rents some grouse moors beyond.

The Dee acts like a moat; I could recall it more clearly than the castle. It had a hypnotic quality. Water from the Cairngorms, chilled by melting snow, swept triumphantly over smooth grey rocks and shingle beds, with a flurry of spume where boulders were too large to be overswept. The eyes turned from the river to trees that clogged every scene. Trees and shrubs hemmed the main drive leading to the castle—a drive that took a sharp turn, as though to cheat the inquisitive. More languid viewing of Balmoral was possible from some of the hilltops and also from the road that struggled gamely out of Deeside to the north, heading for the upper Don, Tomintoul and the Spey. Only then I could not take my eyes from Lochnagar!

Profuse nature is Balmoral's defence against the prying eye, yet the story of royal associations with Balmoral, right down to the present day, is one of cordial informality. And when the Queen and her family are not in residence, the grounds of the castle are open for viewing at prescribed times. One might also use the woodland paths through Ballochbuie and pass close to *garbh allt*, the rough burn, where it spills down the hillside as the Falls of Garravalt. From a bridge strung across the gorge above the foaming water, royal visitors and their guests could contemplate a view of Beinn a' Bhuird before scurrying home for tea. Wander through Balmoral grounds and you will be excited by some of the sculpture. A gargantuan wild boar must have been inspired by Prince Albert. Set on grassland with the pinewoods round about, the boar hints that Continental influences were at work in the development of this royal estate.

The spirit of Albert broods heavily over Balmoral. He was a rather shy man who relaxed most easily when only his family was present. Albert, no doubt infected by the Puritan ethic that work exalteth a man—that "the Devil finds work for idle hands" —was theoretically on holiday at Balmoral. He had a restless mind and itchy fingers, demolishing the castle he found and setting another in its place. Albert was a forester extraordinary and also modernised the farms.

Victoria is remembered mainly as she was portrayed by the early photographers—a sad-faced, dumpy, black-clad figure. The best-known picture is that showing her on a pony being held by the tall, kilted John Brown who, following Albert's death, was Victoria's confidant for over twenty years. This photograph, and others of the period, do not flatter the Queen. They show Victoria, the widow, everlastingly grieving over the death of Albert, which occurred when he was only 42 years old. Through Victoria, Britain's favourite colour became black. Her pose was a queenly pose in that age before Royalty was permitted to relax in public. In any case, relaxation was not possible in the pioneering days of photography, when excruciatingly slow emulsions made long exposures a necessity. Indoors, the head of a sitter was clamped in position, the evidence of the clamp being 'touched out' at the negative stage.

Was Victoria like the woman on the photographs, even in widowhood? She was once, of course, young and impetuous. Albert's sudden death drove her to the brink of madness. There is enough in her Highland journals to indicate a zest for life—and particularly for Deeside, where she and Albert had been happiest. She cannot have always looked glum.

Deeside folk remembered her as a person who became more Scottish than the Scots. Her Deeside mansion, with its tartans of Hunting Stewart, was like a stage set for a drama written by Walter Scott. There was even a Balmoral tartan designed by Albert—a pattern of black, red and lavender on grey. Thistle motifs and stuffed deer heads were other features to be seen at Balmoral. This Highland palace became a microcosm of the Scottish way of life as imagined by romantics. Infected by Balmoralism, better-off folk began to wear bonnets known as Balmorals as they attended the Highland games.

Victoria and Albert had their first joyous views of the Highlands in 1842. Each was 23 years of age, "young and happy". The Marquis of Breadalbane welcomed them to Taymouth Castle (by the mouth of Loch Tay, not the river). Knowing that Albert had a love for guns, Breadalbane mustered three hundred men to flush out game, and the day's bag consisted of nineteen roe, some hares and pheasants and three brace of grouse.

In September 1847 the Royal couple journeyed to the western side of Scotland. They sailed to Oban and the islands and were driven through Glencoe. Albert travelled further north to attend a meeting, and the Queen was ensconced at Lord Abercorn's house at Ardverikie on Loch Laggan. The Glencoe sortie was undertaken when the weather was "excessively cold and showery", and at Laggan every cloud was dark grey, every stream a torrent and the ground squelchy underfoot.

Victoria generously allowed that the country was very fine, "but the weather most dreadful". When the holiday ended, the royal yacht made heavy weather on the southward voyage. Yet

Scotland had already impressed Victoria, and it was "dear Scotland" she glimpsed as the red cliffs of the Mull of Galloway, the country's most southerly point, receded from view.

Reports reached royal circles of a drier, more congenial climate in Deeside. As the rain lashed the royal party at Glencoe and Laggan, Deeside basked in sunshine. The son of Sir James Clark, Queen's physician, had been staying with Sir Robert Gordon at Balmoral. Sir James, and the Earl of Aberdeen, who was Sir Robert's brother, hearing the young man's reports recommended that Victoria and Albert should stay on Deeside. Balmoral was available when Sir Robert died suddenly in 1847, and the couple stayed here for the first time in the autumn of 1848.

Deeside is not an arid desert. Rain does fall here. R. L. Stevenson, who spent the wet summer of 1881 in the valley, commented that "the countryside is delightful, more cannot be said; it is very beautiful, a perfect joy when we get a blink of sun to see it in. The Queen knows a thing or two, I perceive; she has picked out the finest habitable spot in Britain."

To the Queen, in the first raptures, "the scenery is wild, and yet not desolate, and everything looks much more prosperous and cultivated than at Laggan. The soil is delightfully dry." Victoria and Albert strode beside the Dee, "a beautiful rapid stream which is close behind the house. The view of the hills towards Invercauld is exceedingly fine." The castle had "a picturesque tower and garden in front, with a high wooded hill; at the back there is a wood down to the Dee; and the hills rise all around". Red stags "come down of an evening quite near to the house".

Victoria and Albert, with their young family, were at Balmoral for three weeks, with the Queen prattling to her diary and the Prince enthusing about scenery that reminded him of his native Thuringia. They returned to Balmoral in the autumns of 1850 and 1851. In the following year, Albert negotiated with the Fife trustees and bought the property for £31,500, at the same time leasing the adjoining Abergeldie.

Now they had their own Highland retreat, which was to be modified to their own tastes. Sir Robert Gordon had demolished and rebuilt an old Farquharson house at Balmoral, and now Albert had the Gordon edifice torn down. In its place rose the present castle, its architect being William Smith, of Aberdeen. I suspect that the restless, imaginative Albert was free with his ideas. Was it Victoria's idea that there should be some tartan linoleum?

The new owners, entering the house for the first time, had an old shoe tossed after them "for good luck". In due course, some of the walls were hung with sporting pictures by Landseer and portraits by Winterhalter. Wrote Victoria, with justifiable exaggeration: "All has become my dear Albert's own creation, own work, own building, own laying out, as at Osborne: and his great taste and the imprint of his dear hand have been stamped everywhere."

Victoria, diarist, set down her impressions of Highland scenes and accounts of Highland adventures in a schoolgirlish prose, adorned by simple water-colour sketches. She wrote for her own enjoyment, and that of the people in her immediate circle. It was suggested that she might publish her notes, hence the *Journal*, which has its limitations as literature but continues to enchant us.

At Balmoral, this retreat from the stuffy court circles, formality was at a minimum. Grenville, writing in 1849, expressed his dislike of courts and all that appertained to them, but he was glad to have made an expedition to Deeside "and to have seen the Queen and Prince where they certainly appear to great advantage". He added that Balmoral was pretty, the house small. "They live there without any state whatsoever; they live not merely like private gentlefolks, but like very small gentlefolks, small house, small rooms, small estabishment."

No royal guard was present. There was just a solitary policeman, "who walks about the grounds to keep off impertinent intruders or improper characters. . . . They live with the greatest simplicity and ease. The Prince shoots every morning, returns to luncheon, and then they walk or drive. The Queen is running in and out of the house all day long; often goes about alone, and walks into cottages, sits down and chats with the old women."

William Simpson, who had been a war artist in the Crimea, stayed with his friend the Prince of Wales at Abergeldie and recalled that the day before he left the Prince went deer-stalking; he took Simpson with him. "We first drove in a trap past Balmoral, where we met the Queen walking on the grass. The Prince stopped the trap, and I remember that the conversation was about President Garfield (just then assassinated). The Queen had had a telegram that morning announcing his death, and the two royal personages spoke very feelingly about the event."

Victoria was not allowed to forget her position as Queen. Red despatch boxes arrived from Westminster. Statesmen came wheezing up the steps at Balmoral after having spent fourteen hours in trains and making the final approach to Balmoral in carriages. Frequently they arrived at the door to find that the Queen was out on one of her jaunts. She was no stay-at-home and picnicked by burn and loch and took long pony rides into the hills, developing a passion for climbing mountains. She and Albert even travelled incognito to distant places.

Victoria had become devoutly Scottish. On the 1850 holiday she attended Highland games at Braemar castle, joyously watching stone-putting, hammer-throwing, caber-tossing and racing by ghillies. When an open air ball was held at Corriemulzie in September 1852, the Queen insisted that Albert wore the full sartorial trimmings, her dress being ordinary, grey but enlivened by a plaid stole. There were sixty revellers, dancing to the strains of seven bagpipes in the light of torches held by sixty Highlanders!

Whole days given over to family outings. Once dear little Victoria (who, then known as Vicky, would grow up to become the mother of Kaiser Wilhelm II) sat on a wasp nest, was stung several times and had to be rescued by Donald Stewart. The Queen was too alarmed to do anything but cry out.

The Queen took to the high hills on the back of a Highland pony. It may have been a dun-coloured animal, which is far and away the most numerous. A friend who analysed the stud book of the Highland Pony Society found that duns accounted for about 67 per cent of the entries. They were so common, indeed, that a fine classification had developed—blue dun, grey dun, dark dun, golden dun, smokey dun. Of the remaining animals, grey was in the majority. Black was the least common. And my friend—who will travel scores of miles to see an unusual pony —is still looking for a chestnut. He does not believe it exists.

The reins of Victoria's pony were held by John Brown, who had been a stable boy at the time of the first royal visit. He could walk reputedly at over five miles an hour without showing undue fatigue. His tread, according to Victoria, was "vigorous" and "light elastic". If a picnic was planned, a pony was delegated to carry the provisions—hampers, plaids and the billycan.

The men of Deeside introduced the visitors to the remotest areas. Victoria and Albert were directed to Ben Macdhui, from which they could look down on the Wells of Dee. It had been a disappointing outing up the side of Scotland's second highest peak, for a cloying mist lay around the Cairngorms. Eventually the visitors felt a wind on their faces, the mist was dissipated and they had their panoramic view. They deserved it. So rough was the track to the plateau that the Queen had frequently to dismount and walk. She was told that the spring water on the hill was too cold to be drunk by a lady, and so she had whisky and water from a flask. For a lady, Victoria was very partial to whisky.

The last part of the return journey to Balmoral was by moonlight. Most of the company scurried to their beds, but Victoria confided the events of the day to her diary, writing: "Never shall I forget this day or the impression this very grand scene made upon me; truly sublime and impressive; such solitude." When the writing was finished, she doubtless planned the next jaunt!

The royal obsession with hills irritated some of the guests at Balmoral, especially members of the Government for whom a turn round Hyde Park would be more than enough. Mr Glad-

stone was an exception. He did not mind hill-walking, though
he undertook it without show of enthusiasm. Gladstone was
inclined to take his pleasures seriously. During a visit in 1884
he was driven to Derry Lodge and ascended Ben Macdhui on
foot. The statesman wrote of Deeside itself: "This place is on
the whole very beautiful and satisfactory, and . . . has lost for
me none of its charms, with its black-green fir and grey rock,
and its boundless ranges of heather still almost in full
bloom."

In early September 1860, came the first of the Royal progresses
during which Victoria and Albert concealed their identities.
Lady Churchill and General Grey were their principal com-
panions. Leaving Balmoral they took a leisurely course up the
valley to Braemar (where their horses were changed) and pressed
on to the Linn of Dee, crossing the river by a new bridge. The
party entered the wilderness in Glen Geldie (where there was
another change of horses) and went on to Speyside, seeing *en
route* a number of red deer and hearing the shots of men who
were out stalking.

In those days, one crossed the Spey by ferry. West of the
river, a barouche was hired for the royal couple, who found the
outfit shabby and uncomfortable. Lady Churchill and the
General followed in a brake driven by John Brown. It was dark
when they reached Grantown-on-Spey and, still keeping their
anonymity, they booked accommodation at a hotel. Supper consisted of mutton broth, "hodge podge", chicken with white
sauce, roast lamb and potatoes, plus cranberry tart. Victoria and
Albert were directed into a small bedroom that contained a large
four-poster bed.

Next morning was grey, with low cloud and drizzle. They
called on Lord Seafield at Castle Grant, admiring the many
species of pine he had planted in the grounds. Returning to the
village, they found a reception committee. Someone had recog-
nized the visitors. The journey was resumed as soon as possible,
across the moors to Tomintoul and on to Balmoral. The sun was
setting as they descended into Deeside, which meant that they

must have stopped to admire Lochnagar. A fortnight later, still incognito, they set out for Invermarsk and Fettercairn.

Victoria wished "we could travel about in this way and see *all* the wild spots in the Highlands". She was always wishing. In mid-September 1859, as another Balmoral holiday ended, she wished that "we might be snowed up and unable to move. How happy I should have been could it have been so"!

When, at the age of 42, she lost her mother, was then widowed—and driven half-mad with grief—Deeside became her main solace. She who symbolised power and Empire, who presided over the richest nation in the world, spent a third of each year in simple Highland pleasures.

Linn of Muick

Tomintoul

The Cairngorms from the road between Tomintoul and Speyside

16

REFUGE IN GLEN MUICK

A man who stood near the main gate at Balmoral winced at my pronunciation of Muick, which was as spelt. He told me to travel six miles down the road leading to Ballater, and then turn right. "Ye'll soon find Glen Mick." Queen Victoria had doubtless learnt to cope with the pronunciation but she had a habit of writing down the name as "Muich".

Balmoral, on that winter day, looked cheerless, broody under heavy cloud. A wind was zipping around the dark masses of the trees. I preferred, at that chilly moment, to think of summer days, with the woodland lighter, livelier—one hundred and fifty shades of green to offset the solemnity of the pines, and broom to give the roadside a carnival atmosphere, blossoming to blotch the whole district with yellow.

Initially, the way to Glen Muick was beside the rented lands of Abergeldie. I saw heather and a stubble of young conifers. These trees would, in due course, blot out most of the light by growing in the mass, all at the same age, to be swept away as so much vegetable fibre when they had reached early middle age. Foresters would then simply heel in another crop. I was presuming, of course, that this was commercial plantation. Given a chance to grow over about one hundred years, the conifers—or those that survived—would have lost the neat pyramidical forms of adolescence and have become giants of individual shape and character.

K

At rather more than six miles from Balmoral I took a right turn to pass down a narrow road fringed by birches. They were more pleasing to behold than conifers in the mass. No-one had planted them. If three *birks* are lined up, there must have been an accident! Here, gayly informal, was a collection of interesting tree characters. Birches are short-lived but soon become gnarled and lichen-plated; they decorate a scene without dominating it.

A local man instructed me how to reach the main road up the glen. It seems that I had turned to the right a little too soon. At the moment I was on a public road, but the man was at pains to tell me about an off-shoot, royal route to the upper glen, which is private. That way went Victoria and Albert in a carriage drawn by horses—traversing ten miles from Balmoral to a refuge by Loch Muick. It became a sort of Shangri-la.

Ten miles, with a climb of only three hundred feet, does not qualify as Scotland's most epic journey. Could Glen Muick give the royal visitors much privacy? The difference in character between the two places is radical. The sense of isolation is heightened by the fact that wheeled vehicles must return by the same route, discouraging tourists. Beyond Muick are only footways, zig-zagging up the slopes. There was also royal delight in being beside the largest sheet of water in the area—a 550-acre loch, lapping and fretting in a basin at an elevation of 1,311 feet. In a curious way, Loch Muick gives the impression of great depth to those who have no idea what the true depth is. Perhaps it is because hills seem to plummet into the water. There is the same effect at Wastwater, in the Lake District.

I saw—and ignored—the private road, but I was still thinking about it and the traffic that used it when I encountered a corner leading to a constricted zig-zag, where I frenziedly yanked the driving wheel this way and that. Within minutes I had turned on to the road that would deliver me to near the head of the glen. The road unfolded in long, fairly straight lengths, which was consoling, for it was wide enough for one car but rather too narrow for vehicles to pass each other at speed. Early warning of approaching traffic was vital. A deep tyre mark imprinted on the verge indicated where someone had tried to make two go into one.

I was intrigued by the name Muick. Most Highland place-names are Gaelic, and this word in origin is said to mean 'mist'—presumably the Scottish variety. The mouth of Glen Muick has been planted with trees that are still young, a forest kindergarten. The scenery became grander, and soon there were odd 'black' trees, the pines, dotted about or genially grouped near a river that was now creaming over the Linn o' Muick.

Across the river lay the route taken by royalty—straight, level, undeviating, and—as far as I could see—devoid of passing places. The road seemed to be on a ledge cut from the hillside; and trees stood to attention on either side for most of the way. Once that carriageway was the setting for a mishap involving the Queen. On a dark night in 1863 Victoria was making a late return to Balmoral from Muick when the driver of the carriage lost his sense of direction; the carriage bumped across some rough ground and overturned. The Queen, slightly injured, was rescued by John Brown, but it was necessary to bandage her head. She later had only a light supper, "a little soup and fish in my room", before going to sleep.

There had been no Albert to console her; he died in 1861. Did Victoria return again and again to the head of Glen Muick to be near her late husband in spirit? She would recall some of the bright events of the past: picnics at the delta, where later a shiel used by deer-stalkers would be developed into a substantial house; a meal of cold food after a scramble up the two miles of the Glassallt path to the Dubh Loch, and days when Albert was elated at having shot stags. Then Glen Muick was relatively bare, its afforestation dating from 1870.

Inevitably, there were experiments at crossing native hinds with stags introduced to 'improve' the strain. Sir Allan Mackenzie acquired a stag that was the progeny of a wapiti bull and a red deer hind. The captive beast was introduced to hinds gathered on the local hills. Another unsuccessful experiment involved Warnham Park blood. Since 1914, nature has been allowed to take its course.

Glen Muick opened out into what looked like a soggy plain, where the austerity of the scene was moderated a little by neat stands of conifers. Presumably, long years ago, there once were beavers in the Deeside area, and possibly some of those beavers laboured at the head of Glen Muick, where conditions would be right for them to build dams and lodges. At that time elk would emerge from cover to wade in the shallows and graze on water lilies. Were there wolf packs in this area? Wolves survived in the Highlands long after the species was extinct in England, and Glen Muick was sufficiently wild and remote to give them sanctuary. At the end of the fifteenth and the start of the sixteenth centuries, wolves were "increasing at an alarming rate", but man began to win the battle against them. By 1620, over £6·50 was being paid for a wolf skin which was a measure of the scarcity.

I cannot recall in detail the final stages of the motor run to the head of the glen, through what Victoria considered to be "real severe Highland scenery". Lochnagar took and held my eyes. When the road had burst from the shadow of crags and trees beyond the Linn I saw some of the bastions of Lochnagar, and the plain moorland no longer satisfied me as scenery.

Seen from Glen Muick, Lochnagar resembled a ridge tent with three poles, around which the 'canvas' sagged. The tops of the spires gleamed white or silvery under the fretful clouds. Lochnagar has a dozen points extending upwards to beyond the 3,000-feet contour, and the highest of them is Cac Carn Beag, at 3,786 feet, seen clearly by knowledgeable travellers using the main road in Deeside.

Lochnagar looked deceptively simple of construction. Its outlines were clear-cut. It does have a variety of features that is seen only by those who trudge across it. On Lochnagar are majestic, ice-plucked corries; rock faces that soar up for hundreds of feet; and lochs that on dull days, by retaining a sparkle, look like eyes set in deep sockets. This hill has a staggeringly large size, sprawling over sixty square miles. Now it seemed to be showing its teeth—craggy 'teeth' that were the precipices. Lower down, pines stood in their neat blocks, like telegraph poles topped by green plumes.

How well did Victoria and Albert know Lochnagar—or Beinn Cichean as once it was known, alluding to the 'teats' or paps, the several peaks? They climbed it, of course, and the first time was a day or two after their initial arrival on Deeside. Albert found amusement in shooting red grouse and ptarmigan. They visited the Dubh Loch. Eventually the Queen, not content with writing the *Journal*, had important events recorded on stone. Lochnagar's lower slopes became littered with her inscribed cairns.

On the first Royal ascent of Lochnagar, Victoria must have felt that bad weather had followed them from Laggan. (Did she ever go out on a warm and sunny day?) Mist had settled on the shoulders of the hill like a grey shawl. The weather became "cold, wet and cheerless". It was brighter on the second expedition. The royal party paid autumnal visits to their Highland home, and therefore missed much. They did not know the Lochnagar of deep winter, when its shoulders were padded with corries of snow. Nor did they apparently have experience of Lochnagar in spring, when the ptarmigan were croaking and the dunlin trilled and golden plover whistled from the peat hags.

The public road up Glen Muick ended with a flourish at a rough car park that violated the integrity of the scene. A wintry silence endured between the dark hills. I was not far from the site of the Spital of Glen Muick, a hospice at which the traveller could find overnight board and refreshment. When the Spital closed, it was succeeded by an inn, which in turn closed in 1846, so Victoria and Albert would not remember it as a going concern. Good modern roads through the major glens siphoned the traffic from the old hill tracks that were used for centuries. Each autumn, the echoes in Glen Muick were raised by lowing cattle

being driven in large herds to the trysts at which they were purchased by the English graziers. Men have written of 'black'
cattle. Some of the cattle would indeed be black, but in the Highlands 'black' was also synonymous with 'rough'.

I strode along the path beside Loch Muick until I could see
the massed pines marking the site of the new shiel Victoria had
built at this, her most private retreat. The rooms she occupied
overlooked the water. Pines planted at the time are now over a
century old, restricting the views from the building. The open-
ing, on 1st October 1868, was marked by a fairly informal
house-warming at which whisky-toddy was served. There were
Highland reels. Victoria retired and did not object when the
revelry continued in the steward's room.

Occupying one of the upper rooms was the faithful John
Brown, a man who had enjoyed the friendship of Albert and, for
these past four years, had been the Queen's personal attendant.
He revered her—and the memory of Albert. The Prince had
spent part of his Highland holidays learning Gaelic from the
ghillies, and John Brown, as though reciprocating on behalf of
his kinsfolk, slowly mastered German, the Prince's old tongue.
Eight years younger than the Queen, John Brown stood out in a
crowd. He was tall, red-haired, bearded, and so assertive that
when he sensed that Gladstone's prattling was boring the
Queen, he gave the statesman a nudge, and declared, "Ye've
said enuf!" Rumour had it that he had spoken gruffly to the
Queen, calling her "wummun"! Rumours were, indeed,
commonplace about the relationship between the Queen and her
personal attendant. She was slyly referred to at times as Mrs
Brown.

Returning down Glen Muick to the car park I saw walls composed of rounded grey stones, laid together dry, without mortar.
The silence of the afternoon was broken gruffly by a hooded
crow, its body swaddled in French grey feathers but its wings
black. Around Deeside you might see carrion and hooded crows,
and inter-breeding is known. Apart from the obvious differences
in the colour of the body plumage, there are distinctions

between the two types of crow in the choice of nesting sites. The hoodies tend to nest on rock ledges, while carrion crows favour single trees or small copses on the hill. At long last, scientists have sorted out the relationship between the two. Once they were counted as separate species, the hoodie as *Corvus cornix* and the carrion crow as *Corvus corone*. They are being accepted as conspecific.

Unlike the gamekeepers and shepherds of the Highlands, I do not hate crows and, indeed, have a sneaking admiration for their robust form and great intelligence. I do not rear game birds or have the supervision of sheep. A pair of crows will quarter a moor systematically, seeking the eggs and young of the birds. At lambing time crows might pluck the eyes from a still living lamb that has been born weak or ailing or is one of a set of twins. I have seen the pathetic effects of such attacks, but surely only a rogue element of the crow population is responsible.

A foot and a half in length, finely proportioned, with strong bill and a stubble of fine hair around the base—almost as if the bird had forgotten to shave that day!—the crow still impresses me as a bird finely attuned to life in the twentieth century, thriving in the face of shotgun pellets, rifle bullets, poisoned bait, traps and the pokers used to dislodge crow nests, their eggs or young.

In the late afternoon, with a rising wind to give the promise of a stormy night, I stared through the murk of Glen Muick without seeing another sign of life. This is not to say that the area was desolate. A Highland winter has its surprises.

The resident of a remote house on the hills was surprised when he left some household rubbish in a bin. Strands of bacon hung out and were visited by a blue tit that dined greedily. So the householder strung some suet from the clothes line. Next day there were half a dozen titmice to be seen. To reach the house the birds had crossed a mile or two of open ground.

I motored in to Ballater, with memories of Glen Muick tucked away in the lockers of my mind. Some of those memories came tumbling out when a holidaymaker, like myself a comparative newcomer to the district, asked me where I had been. "Glen Mick," said I, and was asked, politely, "Don't you mean Glen Mewick?"

He, poor tourist, would also have to learn!

17

QUOTH THE RAVEN

The raven did not so much fly as walk from the crag into space and let the uprushing air carry it high. When it was near the torn edges of the clouds the bird called, dryly and deeply—"pruk, pruk." I had to restrain myself from cheering. It was the first raven I had seen on Deeside.

Where was the bird's mate? With ravens, the pair bond endures from one season to the next. I have seen groups of ravens that were not true flocks, for within the group the pairs were clearly distinguished. Was the raven I saw a youngster brought here by the westerlies—wafted, for instance, from the Monadhliath, beyond the Spey?

The raven hung about the area, offering me some distinctive silhouettes. Its large pick-axe bill was clear to see. The bird barked again and veered away, still powered by the wind rather than a beating of its wings. Ravens are almost as clever as buzzards at using the flow of the air. I have seen a large flock disporting on the thermal currents, diving and cork-screwing, as though they were simply enjoying the experience. Once a raven turned upside down and glided for a considerable distance, showing off before me.

Visit hill country often enough, and hear enough raven talk, and you become a mimic, barking at the birds as they rise from some shattered crag, and being amused at their response. The strong, dark, slightly sinister raven flies sternly away when the deception has been exposed.

The majority of British ravens live in the misty west and have a sixth sense that tells them where carrion is to be found. Using the size and strength of its enormous beak, a raven makes a quick incision in the body of some dead creature and takes in gobbets of rank flesh. Birds on the coastal cliffs descend to the shoreline and dine on anything remotely edible that has been washed up by the tide.

Highland ravens have little cause to trust man, who has been their persecutor for centuries. Gamekeepers, proud of their prowess, and anxious to display it, strung up the corpses of their victims. Ravens were frequently on display. In a most famous vermin book—that for Glen Garry, Inverness-shire—475 ravens were recorded as having been destroyed between Whitsunday 1837 and Whitsunday 1840.

The Welsh respect their ravens more, maybe because—like the people—ravens have been forced by events into tenanting the wild west of the country, to which they have had to cling tenaciously. Replacement birds for the small colony kept at the Tower of London are invariably taken from Welsh nests. In the Lake District, another prime area for British ravens, persecution was relentless for many years, but ravens are common enough today. Lakeland, indeed, has the majority of the English raven population.

Why should ravens be scarce in Deeside—and, indeed, on the Cairngorms? The landscape might have evolved to cater for their special needs. Generally, ravens are scarce, if not absent, from the east, but the Cairngorms surely extend the raven type of country over the main watershed. Yet a raven nest on the Cairngorms is as uncommon as that of the snow bunting. Ravens appear in numbers here and in the Dee valley only when there is a surfeit of food.

In westernmost Britain, dead sheep sustain the raven. Animals that have died from the many odd ailments that afflict sheep are fair game. The raven even lags its nest with sheep wool. What

Deeside offers the raven are *grallochs* from the stags being stalked and shot in autumn and the hinds that are culled in the winter. This plentiful repast is spread over the time of year when food is generally scarce.

Slain deer are *gralloched* on the spot. The hills become littered with the soft parts of the animals. Some subtle communications system informs ravens from afar where there is plenty of fresh food, and a big influx of birds takes place. The ravens, joining the feast, have the company of golden eagles, buzzards and even foxes. Was it Shelley who wrote of "the obscene Raven, clamorous o'er the dead"?

Dear old MacGillivray heard about the commuting ravens. He was told by a Mr Cuming that large numbers of birds appeared at Braemar, apparently coming from the west, when the game season was in progress. The birds were "attracted by the offal left on the moors when deer are killed".

The Cairngorm area is mainly one of grouse moor and deer forest, with few sheep, and so here the ravens are beneficial, clearing up the ground, disposing of the animal tissue in which various insect pests might otherwise lay their eggs. One can understand why the sheep-man dislikes the raven. He associates the bird with mortality within his flock. Pennine shepherds, coming across a mutilated sheep, would kill it, remove the valuable skin and leave the body for the ravens, reasoning that, having food for a number of days, the ravens would not trouble other sheep at that time.

The incidence of ravens killing sheep must be few in number and may be confined to those birds that are immature or non-breeders. Incidentally, another way in which the raven uses the sheep is to pluck, from sheep droppings, the dor beetles that have emerged from eggs laid there.

Norse settlers on the western coasts a thousand and more years ago reverenced the raven. The bird can inspire awe. It has dark and craggy arenas in which to enact the ancient rituals of display and breeding. Then the bird itself is so black, satanic even—black from the tip of its immense beak to the legs on which it struts around the crags. Clearly revealed at close quarters is a black 'beard', as the patch of pointed feathers adorning the front of the neck appears to be. What the raven-watcher does not see as he beholds a bird soaring on the wind is a fine sheen on the feathers—blue and purple on its upper parts, with some green on the underside of the body.

Ravens are amorous long before the countryside has shrugged off winter. In their flightings they display long, wedge-shaped tails. The pick-axe beaks that tugged at animal offal are now employed in picking material for the nest—a large nest, its outer part formed of twigs, the centre lined with softer material, sheep wool perhaps, which acts like an eiderdown when the helpless young must face up to the rigours of a snow or sleet storm. A raven nest is easily seen but reached with difficulty, except by the men who climb in the Highlands and, unwittingly, disturb the birds.

At some time in its nesting programme the sitting bird has to flick snow from its wings. A friend, Bill Robson—an authority on Pennine birds—found a nest that had actually been built on snow, and the instability of the foundations was demonstrated when there was a thaw! The nest I keep under observation is frequently robbed. Sometimes, noticing that once again the eggs are missing, I sit on the edge of the crags with only the impressive twigginess of the structure to admire until the ravens come sweeping by or a bird alights on a crag not far away with a solemn bark, asking me to leave.

A Highland raven is feeding young in April, and with such a good start to the nesting season the young birds are a-wing when some other hill species are settling down to nest. Compared with the young of ground-nesting birds that hatch out covered in down, and scamper about the area shortly afterwards, young ravens are gawky, helpless, repulsive to behold, with stomachs sticking out like drums. In due course, the quills in sheaths droop because they are heavy with blood. The nestlings squabble over food. At first, it is half-digested mush which they coax from within pouches of skin hanging beneath the beaks of the parent birds. A man who squats in a hide hoping to take photographs or make field observations feels sickly at feeding time. The food looks and smells unwholesome. The mutton or deer flesh may already have become rotten when the birds arrived to collect it.

The raven was once generally distributed, and nested with equal zest in trees and on crags. Tree-nesting is becoming more common now that the bird is legally protected and much of the sporting pressure has been relaxed. Gilbert White, the naturalist-parson of Selborne, in Hampshire, gave a classic description of a raven tree he knew as a boy. Each year, the youths of the district attempted to climb the tree and take the raven eggs. They became so frustrated that the tree was felled and "at last, when it gave way, the bird was flung from her nest; and though her parental affection deserved a better fate, was whipped down by the twigs, which brought her dead to the ground".

I have seen a raven nest in a North Country tree. The sight was less pleasing than that of one perched on a ledge on the crags. These crags were the bird's last resort in the face of per-secution. From them any future colonisation of new areas begins. The law smiles at ravens, but the Highlander harbours his ancient resentment, and scientists continue to foul the environment with poisons. The raven holds its own. Will the Corbie, as it is known in Scotland, soon be nesting more regularly on the Cairngorms?

18

BY WAY OF TOMINTOUL

Having followed the military road northwards from Blairgowrie over the Cairnwell pass to Deeside, I had stood on the Bridge o' Dee near Invercauld, whose fine proportions indicate that the army had a soul as well as a mind. Now I would take in another stage of this military way between Perth and Fort George, near Inverness, travelling from Dee to Spey via Tomintoul. At the approaches to the Lecht, 2,114 feet above sea level, I would reach the second highest point on a classified road in Britain.

Our military history is usually presented as a wearying sequence of battles. More attention might be paid to the role of the soldier as roadmaker. In the Highlands, for instance, improvements made by the army during the eighteenth century opened out the region as never before.

Road-making was a military operation—an answer to the unrest caused by the Jacobite rebellions. Good roads made policing easier in a countryside occupied by unfriendly people, as the Romans had discovered many years before. They would also help any rebellious natives moving in a hurry! The military way that had descended into Deeside for a lyrical spell between two awesome tracts of hill country was an outstanding road, made by scores of men who perspired under a hot Highland sun or stoically remained at their tasks when a winter storm flung rain or sleet.

The grandeur of the Cairnwell pass tends to detract from the route that goes by way of Tomintoul. The difference in elevation at the highest points is only about one hundred feet, and conditions on the two roads in winter can be equally grim. A Ballater man (who, incidentally, told me I must pronounce the placename 'Tomintowl') suggested that I might buy a shovel; if there was any snow in Scotland it was more than likely that it had spilled over the A939.

I recalled how cheerfully the Tomintoul folk I met on the Cairnwell accepted winter conditions. The bad-weather outlet from Tomintoul is northwards, through Dufftown, but this is clearly a waste of time—and petrol—for anyone going to Perth. So the Tomintoul folk motored to Deeside for mile on undulating mile with crisp snow under the car tyres almost the whole time.

A reader will have already gathered that there are several types of Highland winter, affecting different elevations. When the snow dogs howl over the Cairngorms or Lochnagar, the intermediate glens can have a sunny foretaste of spring. As I drank coffee in an elegant room at the Ballater railway station—which was built at the comparatively late date of 1869, with a powder room for the Queen—I pondered on the wild conditions that might even then be affecting the hills at two thousand feet.

Maybe that is why I did not rush to where my chosen road began, inconspicuously, near Crathie church. I recalled the church as it was on my last visit, in tripperish summer. Gaggles of excited holidaymakers had left their cars in a large park between here and the main gate of Balmoral. They found more interest than I had done in this church with a spire, which is a modern history lesson for those with the patience to read inscriptions on memorials. Queen Victoria used the church frequently and no doubt approved of its appearance. The general shape is like a cross, fashioned of gleaming white granite taken from Inver quarry. The roof is of red tiles.

There is around Crathie church that sort of sadness the thousands of visitors to Haworth, in Yorkshire, feel when, having walked up the cobbled main street, they stand before memorials to the Brontës. Some people enjoy feeling sad, but I am not one of them.

John Brown's body lies a-mouldering in one of the Crathie graves. This brusque but faithful attendant of Victoria came into his own during her chilling widowhood. He began in royal service as a stable boy, was promoted to ghillie in 1849 and to the permanent staff at Balmoral in 1851. John Brown predeceased the Queen, and her tributes to Brown were copious.

He was, according to her message attached to a wreath placed on the grave after the interment, a man who had given "loving, grateful, and everlasting friendship and affection". She noted in the *Court Circular* that John Brown had "filled a position of great and anxious responsibility, the duties of which he performed with such constant and unceasing care as to secure for himself the real friendship of the Queen". John Brown's manners had offended many important people. Were they being in part explained when the Queen wrote that he had "all the independence and elevated feelings peculiar to the Highland race"?

Crathie church is a late manifestation of a Christian spirit which, many centuries ago, impelled missionaries to enter these wild parts of Scotland in a bid to save the souls of an equally wild people. Manirus, or Manaire, "travelled painfully among the Highlanders in the upper parts of Mar that he might recover them from the many reminders of idolatry and superstition which, even till then, were to be found among them". I hope, for Manirus's sake, that he did not suffer from bad feet, which would be a real handicap in the Highlands. His 'painful' travels were doubtless those in which he took exceptional pains to spread the Gospel. Did he see evidence of earlier religious fervour in the stones raised by folk who tried to 'tune in' to the wavelengths used by their gods? There are indeed marks on Deeside of the work of man in prehistory.

A disadvantage in using the Tomintoul road from the south is that a traveller is cheated of a view of Lochnagar, the hill with "steep frowning glories" (Byron) that lifts "its mournful spire-

The Tomintoul road in its descent towards the Spey

Loch Muick

Large numbers of greylag geese winter in the Scottish low country

like peaks to the sky" (Gibb and Hay). With the car's bonnet inclined towards the sky on the long haul from Deeside, one does not even get a good sighting of Lochnagar through the rearview mirror. So I stopped the car, stepping into crisp air to see Lochnagar resting firmly on its immensely wide foundations, the lower slopes covered with dark woodland, but the hill's spires white like fangs.

Stopping again a few hundred yards away, I turned over the flattened body of a mountain hare. The underparts were white, with a darker colouration on the upper parts and, at the top of the head, a smudge of brown. A gamekeeper I met near Gairnshiel knew all about mountain hares. About five hundred hares would be slain during a single day's shoot! It depended very much on "the year".

The Gairn river bridge soared high, like a petrified rainbow. Was Highland canniness expressing itself with the remembrance of cloudbursts after which burns and rivers rolled along with devastating effect, and bridges toppled? Floods would never reach the parapet of this one.

The road to Tomintoul was a true moorland road, breasting the ridges, dipping in the hollows, edged by sparse vegetation that had learnt to keep its head low to avoid catastrophe in times of gale Every plant was compact and deep-rooted. There were small stands of pine, and some mature larch, but they kept to the hollows. On the 'tops' the wind ran a comb through the tousled hair of ling, which so plentifully covers the eastern moorlands. Heather grows best between the elevations of 500 and 1,500 feet.

In winter, the heather looked dead, but green shoots were appearing under the sombre canopy of tough stems, as the red grouse knew, for they fed here. I saw grey patches where heather had been burnt off to encourage the growth of fresh shoots, food for sheep and grouse. It is selective burning, with close regard to weather conditions. A man did not simply run berserk with a torch, igniting all in view. Sections were burnt every year so that the heather was of varying ages. A keeper waited for the

L

correct wind strength and a direction that carried the fire to areas already burnt, reducing the risk of setting half the district alight. A fire must not be so savage that it took hold of the peat and smouldered for days if not for weeks. Nothing damages a moorland more than deep incineration.

The moors I saw gave the appearance of being well-maintained. There were innumerable grey patches, clear-burnt areas that looked from a distance like impetigo on the face of the hills, being dull grey under cloud. Stopping the car again I found other common moorland plants. Ling is just one species of heather. In August the bell-heather appears a little ahead of the ling and claims a disproportionate amount of attention.

What could nature do if a plot of this moorland was fenced off? A friend who enclosed 70 acres of moorland, from which most of the heather had been grazed off by sheep, found that within five years the heather had returned to virtually the whole acreage. If he had not arranged for the land to be grazed again, though to a limited extent, it would soon have been sprouting trees. Man therefore debases the landscape by his regular burning of the ling. The end result is almost a monoculture.

The patches of trees on low ground were little more than shelter belts, but then I saw the first of the modern-style forests. It came in sight during the descent to Strathdon, about which—apart from the trees—there was a lush green, a strip of pasture and cultivation between high hills, like a fingermark left by a giant. This agreeable fertility is expressed in an old couplet: "Ae mile o' Don's worth twa o' Dee/Except for salmon, stone, an' tree".

I was 19 miles from Braemar. Tomintoul lay 11 miles ahead.

When the Lecht road was unmetalled, dusty in summer, puddly in winter, the traffic using it varied even more than it does today. Many travellers were pedestrians. Among them, having a job where fitness was essential, were the cattle drovers. In late summer and autumn droves of black cattle raised the dust as they were moved from the northern hills towards the lowlands, and from here into England where, with cattle driven in from Ireland and Wales, they provided the folk of the expanding towns with prime beef.

The drovers should have walked an average of twelve miles a day. The cattle might be moved this distance, but drover and dog were forever on the move, dashing left and right as well as forward as they kept the beasts to the prescribed route. The drovers had to be tough because they lived almost as roughly as their stock. Oatmeal was the staple food of the indomitable men to whom the stretches of hill road via Tomintoul and the Lecht were just a phase in a long journey.

The lore of the droving days is not confined to the Scottish Highlands. In my native Yorkshire I have heard much about the trade. The short, staggy, long-horned animals were known as 'kyloes'. This term is remembered at many of the Pennine farms near old drove roads, having been passed down from generation to generation. It was in May or June that the droves moved through Yorkshire. In the June of 1792, Lord Torrington arrived at Gearstones, a wild spot near the headwaters of the river Ribble, and saw one of two annual fairs for Scotch cattle. Torrington went to the public house, "the seat of misery in a desert, and tho' (unluckily for us) fill'd with company, yet the Scotch fair held upon the heath (there I go to meet Macbeth) added to the horror of the curious scenery; the ground in front crowded by Scotch cattle and drovers; and the house cramm'd by the buyers and sellers, most of whom were in plaids, fillibegs, etc".

What did the Scotsmen make of the accommodation at Gearstones? A visitor in 1861 noted that "the fare is better than the lodging. Three kinds of cakes, eggs, and small pies of preserved bilberries were set before me at tea; but the bed, though the sheets were clean, had a musty smell of damp straw".

Scottish-bred cattle passed over the flatlands of Yorkshire, to the east of the Pennines. There was, according to one report, a proportion of one drover to sixty or seventy beasts, and the drovers carried shoeing-irons to remedy the shoes of any animal going lame between villages. Country blacksmiths could be relied upon to do all the shoeing, and a blacksmith at Langthorpe, near Boroughbridge, is reputed to have hand-made 30,000 'ox-nails' every year and often to have earned £6 a day in shoeing when a Scotch drove came along.

Queen Victoria, during her long autumn sojourn in Deeside, must have seen droves of cattle and noticed, perhaps with some amusement, that each animal wore shoes to protect its feet against the roughness of the roads during an exceedingly long journey.

The sternest test during my swifter crossing of the hills came with an ascent of the Hill of Allargue from Cock Bridge. There was over seven hundred feet of climbing on a road which does not compromise much with the hill by running along contours; it takes the shortest practical line to the horizon. I watched a heavy lorry make a run at the hill, and soon the driver was notching down the gears and resigning himself to a long drag. The vehicle moved upwards with roaring engine, leaving a cloud of blue-grey exhaust fumes.

Flakes of snow falling on the road at over two thousand feet above sea-level melted instantly. The sun showed its face briefly in a sky that was three-quarters full of restless clouds. A beam of light brought a sparkle to insulators on an electricity pylon—one of many of these tall lattice towers marching across the high places with the devil-may-care attitude of soldiers in battle. In low country, the pylon dominates every view. Here, though having the same grand proportion, it was not permitted to take command of the scene, the hills being grander in every respect.

Golden plovers nest on these well-fleshed hills, and some of my best views of birds in their nesting territories have been enjoyed from the car. Drawing off the road, and stopping the engine, I have wound down the windows and listened for the drawn-out, plaintive whistling that seems to be an expression of the very soul of the hills. The calls are low in pitch but in still conditions they carry far. In spring a golden plover, its territories not many yards from the road, stretches up its neck until the bird resembles an old-fashioned wine bottle and eyes me from beside a tussock of grass, around which it trips lightly, to stand alert and call again. A cock bird, spangled with gold and black, is exceeded in sartorial beauty only by the colours of the down on its precocious chicks.

Golden plovers might be seen on the hills before winter has ended, being impatient to be back on the nesting grounds. Serious attempts at nesting do not begin until April. The wintering flocks of golden plover on low ground look pale. The plumage, devoid of the nuptial black, will darken again at the approach of spring, in some cases revealing—by being especially dark—that some of the flocks are composed of non-British nesters. A golden plover seen in winter might be a denizen of our hills during the nesting season or might be faced by an ocean flight to, say, Iceland, as a laggard spring returns to this bleak northern land.

The road at the Lecht had caught the eye of the midday sun and was a ribbon of silvered tarmacadam (or was it asphalt?), descending in a wedge between the 2,500-foot eminences of Meikle Corr Riabhach and Beinn a' Chruinnich. The pass looked less severe than its reputation. Tales I had heard about its condition in winter had terrified me! Stopping for a while on grass that had been dusted with fine snow I had a lingering view of the place where the road to Tomintoul has a sudden wild dip in a lumpy landscape.

Ten minutes later I was surrounded by a more temperate Scotland and following a road that meandered amiably. This district, in comparison with the Lecht, was benevolent, its fields, even its blocks of conifers, being restful to the eyes after the austerity of the hills. There is nothing like a spell in the wilderness to prepare a traveller for the enjoyment of gentler country.

Mountain hares had been familiar to me. Now I surveyed a brown hare, the lowland cousin, from fifteen yards. The hare stood with ears rigidly extended, turning them continuously to pick up the most interesting sounds and meanwhile offering me views of their neat black tips. Why did the hare remain standing? The brown hares I knew at home would have crouched and snuggled down until they resembled old sacking. Or, choosing a moment when the concentration of the observer was broken, would dash away with a superpowered gait.

Tomintoul was an anti-climax. Maybe the weather was to blame for this, having finally made up its mind, opting for sunshine and shower. The sunshine was warm, the showers being of rain, not snow. My feeling of disappointment was a fault neither of the village nor its inhabitants. Knowing of its reputation as the highest village in Scotland I fancifully expected to see an alpine-style settlement, maybe on a ledge of rock overlooking a precipice, with houses built into the hillside and, perhaps, goats or sheep moving down narrow streets with bells jangling from collars! Natives of Tomintoul I have met in various parts of Britain tend to create an impression of a bleak place in a hostile environment.

Tomintoul is high-lying. One informant said the elevation was 1,124 feet above sea level at the square and 1,160 feet at the top of the village. Yet Tomintoul stands on a flattish ground, and when first seen by those who approach it from Deeside it is a huddle of small buildings. The circling hills are rounded, lacking turrets of rock, which to most people signify mountains. The hills do not look to be high. They do not crowd each other or the village. On the day of my visit the dramatic effects created by the hills were extended far up into the sky by soaring white clouds that had silver linings and blue-black underbellies.

The village was neat—in one respect rather too neat for my taste. Trees at the centre had been cruelly pruned and now resembled knobbly walking sticks. None of the villagers— friendly folk all—had snow on their boots, but the postman was using a vehicle with a four-wheel drive, a post-office concession to its servants who maintain rounds in rugged areas. A local man, sensing my disappointment at Tomintoul's apparent lack of wildness, told me that I should turn up in snowtime and see the difference. As one who had crossed the Pennines at 1,200 feet above sea level during a blizzard I could understand his meaning more clearly than, perhaps, a visitor from Kent.

Queen Victoria, who seemed to be pursued about the Highlands by poor weather, came to Tomintoul when there was mist and rain, during one of her long tours during which she tried, with only moderate success, to conceal her identity. She and Albert had an overnight stay at Grantown, with breakfast consisting of porridge, tea, bread and butter. Their plan was to travel, by horse-drawn carriage, up the long drag to Tomintoul, thence by Inchory, Loch Builg and Glen Gairn to Balmoral. Mist extinguished the views, rain kept them from the windows of the carriage, and on the stiff gradient the speed of the carriage was reduced to less than four miles an hour!

Did she actually *see* Tomintoul before moving on to Deeside? Perhaps not. The place is worthy of a special visit. Tomintoul is important as a crossroads just north of the roadless Cairngorms. It receives the Lecht road from Deeside and sends it forward, by way of the Bridge of Brown, to Grantown-on-Spey. It accepts a road from Glen Rinnes and despatches another by Avonside.

I saw the Avon in a heady rush, and thought of its source among the high hills. Sparkling water tumbles from Loch Avon. The water is free of the peat in suspension that gives many a Highland burn the appearance of whisky. Highland folk used to chant, "The water o' Avon it runs sae clear/T'wad beguile a man o' a hunner year," which is just acceptable as doggerel but expresses a truism in easily-remembered form.

Mention of whisky is appropriate in the area round Tomintoul. I told a friend about Glenlivet's vast new conifer forests, mentioning the excellent way in which foresters and farmers co-operated to make the best use of the land. My friend listened impatiently. To him Glenlivet meant only one thing— whisky! When was I going to tell him about that?

If the English of the eighteenth century had kept to their new military road and minded their own business they might have been better received by the native folk. But—being English —they had to interfere with local affairs. At Glenlivet efforts were made to restrict the illicit distilling of whisky. Naturally the locals flouted a law that cut directly across their interests.

Smuggling developed as never before, and it is recorded that "in bands of from 10 to 20 men, with as many horses, with two ankers of whisky on the back of each horse" the smugglers made their way along the banks of the Avon, "singing in joyful chorus". Glenlivet became lawful—and went on to produce large quantities of one of the world's best-known brands of whisky.

The road I was following dipped to the Bridge of Brown, and beyond there was a low-gear crawl to where the way levelled out again. The Cairngorms lay like a stranded school of whales, half a dozen miles to the west. Their fine detail was absent, these smooth hills being toned dove-grey, capped by snow. They commanded respect at a great distance, even when the viewpoint was at half their elevation above the level of the sea.

The road dipped to Speyside between moors which, at first glance, appeared vacant. The 'caretakers' of these winter hills were red grouse, one of which surprised me by perching on a post. I had not previously seen a Highland bird at rest above ground level, though on my native Pennines grouse frequently use the capstones of the dry stone walls as perches. When even the crows, hungered by austerity, move down to the glens the grouse remain in their treeless quarters. After a blizzard just a few tufts of heather or stalks of long grasses protrude from the undulating white desert to sustain the wily moorcocks.

Soon these hills would be animated as the waders moved in to nest. Lapwings show up in the glens as early as February, and from here they spread to the rough grazings. I recalled the exuberant "oo-ips" as cock birds tumbled in the air, pulling out of their dives a moment before I expected them to dash themselves against the ground. Oystercatchers are more prominent in hill conditions. I have seen pairs strutting at the verges of the main road with a startling clarity because their plumage is bright.

Further down the hill was a new plantation, an outlier of the Speyside woodlands. The ground was a tangle of growth over which new-planted conifers would assert themselves. A roebuck bounded across the road, leapt a fence into the plantation and stood watching the car until the deer's nerves became as taut as violin strings, when the animal skipped away.

Grantown had a festive atmosphere. Busloads of skiers were returning from the snowfields, their clothes in dazzling primary colours. Bright young folk from the lowland cities chatter incessantly—as I was to discover on my first entry to the town, and also in the middle of the night. Another busload arrived and disgorged excited and garrulous skiers into the hotel where I had booked a room!

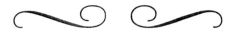

19

MIST OVER CAIRN GORM

Clamber on to the roof of Scotland on any day of the year and you should not be surprised if a snowflake settles on your nose. This circumstance is least likely in summer. Even then it may occur. Patches of snow linger on the Cairngorms the year through, and it is possible to organise a snowball battle somewhere on the hills during Midsummer Day.

In winter, the Cairngorms area is the snowiest part of Scotland. Substantial patches of snow lie above 2,500 feet on about 150 days of the year, a figure that rises to 200 days for the high plateaux. There is money in snow—the money paid by skiers who want winter sports without the expense of travelling to snowfields on the Alps. Many skiers turn up in Speyside simply for the day.

The quality and extent of the snow varies from year to year, but a few enthusiastic skiers pride themselves on being able to ski on the Cairngorms in every month. The main season is reckoned to be from just before Christmas until April, and it is then that the Cairn Gorm chair lift reaches its high peak of popularity, with its capacity to convey about 600 people a day from the Glen More car park to major snowfields.

Devout hill walkers snort at the mention of a chairlift ascent. Most of us cannot resist an easy way up the hill, and the chair lift is valuable as a time-saver. Sitting with dangling legs, a patron using this ingenious device is carried for over a mile and at such an angle that a few minutes later he is about 1,400 feet higher than he was when he sat down. The chairs go on their endless daytime rounds for most of the year, being stopped only when the wind is considered to be too strong for safety. The wind has been known to pluck chairs from the wires.

When I last used the lift I vowed that on my next visit I would walk up the hill. The chairlift was too quick, too efficient for maximum pleasure. Using it, there was a bewildering transition from Glen More, its forest and loch, to the Cairn Gorm barrens. Ideally, one should take the path to the summit and pause now and again—like a diver in compression chambers—to adjust to the changes.

I weakened in my resolve—and rode up the hill using the 'chancy' weather as an excuse. It was, indeed, the type of winter day made for tragedy when a walker goes alone.

The sun warmed up the glens and straths, giving an illusion of early spring, but it was wintry at 1,500 feet. Five hundred feet higher lay mist so thick I could taste it. Mist hung in the air, still and clammy, like vapour in an old-fashioned kitchen on washday.

That day began for me with an early breakfast at Grantown and a short journey to Nethy Bridge. I realised a minor ambition by seeing a crested tit feeding at a bird table. Nearby Garten was deserted of people now that the ospreys were in their distant winter quarters. A red squirrel scampered across the road at almost exactly the place where I had seen the animal, or one of its parents, cross over on my last visit.

Viewed from near Coylumbridge, the Cairngorms looked drab. There were no definite colours, just washes of murky tones. I last travelled this way in early summer, exulting over the glow of yellow from acres of massed broom, beyond which soared hills of purple and mauve. Glen More was then a caravanner's and camper's glen. Now it had become the preserve of skiers. The road I followed was the Ski Road, made by the county council, who I hope received some award, for as roads go this is superb. (Those who cherish memories of Glen More before the commercialisation of the area will doubtless prefer the district as it was).

When entering the Forest Park, the precise moment indicated by a clang from the cattle grid, I was delighted that the Forestry Commission decided to share a wonderland of forest and loch with visitors. Loch Morlich was glass-smooth. The whooper swans must have moved off to Loch Insh. On the Morlich shore stood a Scots pine, its roots exposed by erosion so that it appeared to stand on stilts.

During the approach to the car park I passed into another sort of world. Wisps of cloud played hide-and-seek around the hills. The first large snowdrift terminated abruptly at the edge of the highway, the prompt clearance of which is a matter of great pride to the roadmen. The ski parties must get through!

The builders of the 500-car parking ground appeared to have made a miniature version of a Cairngorm plateau; or it might have conveniently slipped down the hill. Snow buntings were dining on bread scraps (as at Glen Shee). A reindeer, moving far off, was a solitary figure in the barren landscape.

I felt dowdy when I joined a party of skiers, whose clothes flared red. This gaggle of young folk was engaged in Scotland's oldest topic for conversation—the weather, which was then very poor. Should the ski parties spend good money on the lift if there was little chance of a good run back down the hill?

I looked towards the summit of Cairn Gorm. Beyond the park were patches of snow, with large banks of snow higher up, extending into the heavy bank of mist. One sorrowful skier was told that poor visibility would remain for the rest of the day—maybe even for several days. And he was on a two-day trip from Birmingham!

Being by nature an optimist, and having experience of impenetrable mist that suddenly lifted, like a curtain at the opera, I decided to go farther. There was no queue for the chair-lift. I occupied one of twin chairs, and slipped a hinged piece of wood into place to ensure that I did not fall out. Then I was swung into space.

There had been another time when I seemed to come near to the impression of weightlessness—a descent by bosun's chair of the 340-foot main shaft of Gaping Gill, in Yorkshire, in 20 seconds flat! Then I had moved downwards, with dark, damp rock rushing by until I was passing through a chamber the size of a cathedral, like a spider on a fine thread. On Cairn Gorm I now rose at an angle, into mist, and had a fellow feeling with the astronaut.

For a few hundred yards the chair moved in clear air, cold and damp, as it was in Gaping Gill. I looked down to see pinkish rocks and a sparse and jaded plant life, listening to the tinkle of a burn and the "zit, zit" of a dipper.

When the mist enveloped me I felt to be floating rather than dangling. No more than two pylons could be seen at a time. There were moments, half way between two pylons, when a forward view revealed nothing substantial, the strands of wire extending into nothingness. Below me lay a pearl-white snow-field.

A chair on the downward course passed by mysteriously, without a sound. Its occupant, stiff and white, would surely creak, or even crack, as he clambered from his metal steed at the terminus. A swishing sound below led me to notice two skiers on the ground; they materialised and vanished in the space of a few seconds. Had I imagined them? The sleet settling on my clothes slowly built itself up into a grey mush.

The chairlift journey ended some way from Cairn Gorm's summit (4,084 feet). Mist sustained the oppressive washing-day effect, and the sodden clothes of the skiers gently steamed. Men, women and children stomped around in the mist, all looking cold and miserable. An exception was the small girl on her first outing who, having no memories of brighter days on the hills, chortled happily while slithering for a few yards at a time on a slope that was only just deserving of that term. Her joy was in direct contrast to the mood of her parents, who could recall blue skies, crisp air and dazzling snowfields.

The Ptarmigan Restaurant, oasis in a white desert, had a

design which might have been based on an upturned pudding basin but was robust and entirely appropriate to its wild situation, its elegant curves offering hardly any resistance to the Cairngorm blasts. Large windows gave all-round visibility and, inside, the tables were arranged around a circular service area. If man colonises the moon then the design of the Ptarmigan Restaurant will surely also be appropriate to that arid setting.

The atmosphere outdoors was composed of air and water vapour in roughly equal measures. In the high humidity indoors the windows had faintly misted over through condensation, and looking out I saw a monochromatic world in which the skiers were viewed dimly, as are fish through the glass of tanks at an aquarium.

Skiers stomped into the restaurant, knocking 'snow broth' from their boots and simultaneously boosting the circulation of blood. Wherever a person stood for long, a pool of water formed on the floor. Chapped fingers wrestled with clothes as they sought to find wallets to pay for the food they had ordered. Paper money no longer crinkled. It could not have been more unlike the image of the skier and his world as conveyed by modern advertising.

A visitor had seen a ptarmigan perched on the top of the building, which was therefore aptly named. He also mentioned the sighting of a pack of a dozen or more birds somewhere on the other side of the hill, so I took the Oates-like decision of walking to the summit.

The first slope encountered was immediately outside the door of the restaurant, where a drift had been pounded down until it was as hard as concrete. It was an effort to find the first of the marker sticks that have been reared to indicate the way to the summit cairn in poor visibility. Following the markers was almost as difficult. I dared not lose sight of one post until the next had shown itself.

The world was empty, silent, gloomy, with visibility down to maybe fifteen yards. It only became a real world when my feet grated against rocks. Otherwise I crunched snow at every footfall to the cairn. I willed the mist to lift, but the cloying greyness remained. It infuriated me to know that a few hundred feet above the hill the sky would be clear and sunny. If a wind had sprung up, dispersing the mist, I could have had one of the fairest views in Scotland.

When there is settled weather, skiers on tour go from Cairn Gorm to Ben Macdhui as part of a sixteen-mile round that includes descents of smooth slopes for several thousand feet. This weather was fit for no-one, and I trudged sorrowfully down.

There was a sudden wild hope during the return journey that a pack of ptarmigan was approaching. Or perhaps the *famh*, an ugly little monster, mainly reported in summer, had been roused from hibernation by all the activity. Could it be, indeed, that I was being stalked by the ghostly Grey Man (*Fear Liath Mor*) who had decided on a day's outing from his lair on Ben Macdhui?

I stood, listened and looked around as the sound grew steadily louder. From the mist came two skiers, in line ahead, passing before me like apparitions because the mist had drained them of colour. They were gone from sight in an instant, and I was left with a grudging admiration for those who ski with such confidence in poor conditions.

The mournful throng of folk at the Ptarmigan Restaurant agreed that an improvement in the weather was unlikely. We shuffled to the chairlift, to be borne smoothly down to the car park. More sleet settled on my clothes, building itself up as before into a grey fuzz.

The car park looked as bleak as the plateau I had just left—but the snow buntings twittered as they pecked at scraps of bread.

20

WILD GOOSE CHASE

Motoring southwards to Perth through a cosy sort of landscape
—stuffy, indeed, after life on the high hills—I saw that farmers
were still frenziedly ploughing, turning the good earth "brown
side up", benefiting from the mild and dry winter that enabled
them to take machines on to the land without 'poaching' it.

They did not plough alone. No sooner had a ploughshare
sliced through a piece of ground, and twisted the soil neatly over
as a fissured ridge, than black-headed gulls dived in to feed. Each
dense flock of gulls looked like a lowland snowstorm, but that is
where the similarity ended. Each bird was in raucous voice,
bickering with its neighbours, so eager to be first to feed that it
ran the risk of becoming half-buried in the tumbling red earth.
There was little the farmer could do about the noise, but he
would surely go home with jangling eardrums.

A gull that had eaten its fill drifted away to join the white
carpet of gulls settled in the next field. Here the bird would
preen and doze away more of the tranquil day. Hardly any fields
remained green, but in one of the undisturbed tracts were more
substantial birds than the screaming white scavengers on the
ploughlands.

A flock of greylag geese scythed grass, hardly in peace, but
far enough away from the roaring tractor to be comfortable.
Ranged in line formation, about 120 yards from the road, the

geese looked ash-grey against the greensward. They were indifferent to another major noise—the whine and whoosh of road traffic.

I stopped the car without causing a squeak, but the geese saw me. The single birds that had been looking around at the moment I braked acted as sentinels for the flock, standing with necks held stiffly upwards. The movement and pose alerted neighbours who had been feeding. Over two hundred greylags eyed me with their cold sub-Arctic eyes and I heard the first anxious calls—"aahng, aahng"—evoking memories of winter days on the marshes.

The greylag, ancestor of the domestic geese, is easily distinguished from the other 'grey geese' when seen at close range. It has a palish plumage, stout orange-yellow bill and legs that are fleshy in tone. Goslings reared at wildlife parks grow up to develop a ready informality with man and have made the greylag a bird well-known to townsfolk.

The farmyard birds may have become finely-bred for their flesh but some retain enough of the plumage colouration of the wild stock to be recognisably of greylag descent. A friend who reintroduced greylags as breeding birds to a region in northern England lost many of the early nests because farmers collected the eggs, hatched them out, reared the goslings and, in due course, used these birds to improve their decadent goose stocks!

At one time every farmer kept a few geese for sale at Christmas. An English visitor to a collective farm in a Communist country saw 600,000 geese being reared and was told that the stock, at its breeding nucleus, was a mere fifty thousand or so! Each winter, Scotland plays host to about that number of greylags. Their breeding areas are in the lowlands of Iceland. A few greylags fly farther south, into England, but the greylag is primarily a Scottish goose; it arrives at its favoured wintering grounds in about October and stays until about April. Greylag did not become extinct as a Scottish nesting species. Breeding in a feral state occurs in several parts of Britain. It is believed that the Icelandic geese do not mix with birds of British origin.

The life of a wintering greylag appears to us to be idyllic,

M

periods of feeding being followed by periods of roosting, with the bird having the leisure to make a really good job of its preening. In fact, wintering geese face many hazards. Birds are peppered by the fowlers' shot. Experts go for clean kills, but there is a type of hunter known on the coast as the 'marsh cowboy' who is not selective, firing in the general direction of geese in the hope of hitting some.

Winter on the lowlands, where greylags sojourn, is rarely grim. The greylag is, however, a robust bird that can stand for hours on some lonely mudflat or marsh, facing an icy wind without feeling the chill. Birds shot at first light, after roosting through a bitterly cold night, had slivers of ice on their backs! Death befalls some geese more insidiously, from poisons sprayed on the fields to eliminate unwanted plants or insect pests. Scores, if not hundreds of wintering geese, have been picked up dead in the fields. Had the farmers applied killer sprays at too great a strength?

The geese I saw beside the Perth road talked to each other in undertones, debating their next course of action. The vocabulary is not extensive but, with postures, provides geese with an adequate range of expression. As the geese called, the outliers waddled with a haughty gait to join the loose line of birds in a formation that would ensure, if necessary, an ordered lift-off.

Having lost the desire to disturb a large flock of geese just for the fun of seeing them move off in chattering chevrons I left these birds when they seemed to be only seconds away from flight. There would be many other flocks to see in Perthshire, though greylags do not mass to the extent of the pink-footed geese.

My next group of greylags stood in a large field near Scone. The field was between the road and a deciduous wood enlivened by the lingering coppery leaves of beech. Oystercatchers, pied dandies with a very nervous disposition, now on their way to the nesting grounds after wintering at the coast, called shrilly when my near presence excited them. An oyster-catcher cannot whisper!

A cock pheasant displayed its Asian brilliancy in a well-ordered countryside that was so different from the eastern jungles in which its ancestors had evolved. Podgy woodpigeons, ever-hungry, shuffled along with heads well down, and then took flight, their wings slapping together in the air during the initial skyward thrust.

Nine greylags remained standing in the field. One bird was lame. As with the previous group I came under the bright, unblinking goose stare. These statuesque birds had their necks extended, a build-up of tension being indicated by some lateral head-shaking. The greylags became airborne through slow and shallow wing-beats that nonetheless had impressive power. As they lifted off I saw the silver-grey of the forewings contrasting with darker feathers behind.

That evening, beside a quiet upland road near Perth, a game-keeper told me more about geese. He was a veteran who had seen their arrival, sojourn and departure for nearly seventy winters. We spoke in a world that was becoming chilly and dark, composed of browns—woodland browns to our right and, just across the road, where the land dropped in a gentle sweep to the river, the browns of freshly-ploughed arable land. The whole district seemed to glower, as though fearing the night. Only the watercourses far below had real expression, taking light from the sky and passing it back with an added touch of silver.

There were no geese because of the early ploughing, but the keeper had seen land that looked grey with the backs of assembled flocks. In two successive winters a patch of white had been noticed. It was an albino goose, he thought. Itchy-fingered farmers had this year been quick off the mark with tractors and ploughs, and the geese could not feed on raw earth. If I wanted to see a few thousand geese I should "get out Coupar-Angus way", where the keeper had seen a huge flock on the previous day.

I had a consolation prize—a story he told about geese. I was assured that it was quite true. Two elderly men went out goose-shooting, and two geese were killed. There was a big and ungainly bird and one that was smaller, having a light alloy ring about one of its legs. (The goose had been caught and released by someone interested in its future movements. By recovering such rings we have built up a knowledge of the birds' migratory journeys and world distribution).

Courtesy demanded that the older man was given the first choice of goose. He, naturally, selected the smaller bird, which was bound to be younger and more tender than the other. The aluminium ring was detached and sent to the address stamped on it. The old man then plucked and cooked his bird.

After some hours, the goose was still tough, and so it was returned to the oven for a few more hours. The old man still had difficulty in pushing the prongs of a fork into the body, but he ate the bird, which was tough and stringy. In due course, details of the origin and date of the ring he had taken from the goose were sent to him from London. The small goose that held out so much promise of a tasty meal had been ringed in Iceland eight years before.

I heard a sound like a gate swinging on rusty hinges, and looked round to localise it. My gaze returned to the keeper. The wheezy sound was his laughter!

In Perthshire's rich and rolling countryside I should have no difficulty in finding pink-footed geese, for at peak times many thousands of birds inhabit a broad belt extending from Aberdeenshire through Perthshire to Wigtownshire. Pinkfeet are twice as common as they were twenty years ago, and Scotland is their Promised Land in winter, so much so that they are vacating some of the old English haunts.

The largest English concentration of pinkfeet, Solway excepted, is at the mouth of the Ribble estuary. The good folk of Southport see skeins moving to and from—commuting between their feeding grounds and the sandbanks of the estuary on which they pitch at last light for roosting. Southport residents are as familiar with flighting geese as are the folk of Dundee, most of whom now scarcely trouble to look up when a skein passes over.

The pinkfeet wintering in Scotland hatched out in central Iceland and East Greenland. As summer wanes, some Icelandic birds may make the short crossing to Greenland to go through the wing moult before taking a southerly course over the Atlantic for a Scottish landfall. The geese prefer lowland Scotland because it is arable country where, over recent years, there has been a considerable increase in the number of acres devoted to barley.

One evening I motored westwards from Perth under an unbroken expanse of cloud composed of dozens of shades of grey. Rain fell steadily and the visibility was poor. There would be a premature dusk.

A bakery van pressed me hard as I drove, and it would have been folly suddenly to apply my brakes when I had a momentary view of eight grey geese circling a roadside field and pitching down on stubble. They were probably pinkfeet, but I must wait for other circumstances in which to identify the species positively. A pinkfoot has a dark bill banded with pink and a dark head and neck to help distinguish it from the greylag.

Turning off the main road with relief—and receiving a cheerful toot on the horn from the driver of the bakery van!—I followed a steep road to the valley below Dunning. The valley was chequered by patches of green and brown, large fields being strung together by hedges. Here geese could not only find lush grazing but they would have the panoramic views they desired as a safety measure.

Six grey geese rose from a field and passed near a flock of fifty lapwings that was travelling in the opposite direction. Held up by the barrier at a level crossing, I did not mutter dark threats against the railway authorities, the period of waiting being spent watching fifty geese in flight. The birds were in small groups, strung like dark beads against the grey sky, and moving to an area near the village.

Half a mile farther on I came across my first large flock of pinkfeet—maybe five hundred birds, though there could have been twice that number for the valley floor which had looked so flat from a distance consisted here of low rounded hillocks. Many more geese could have been tucked out of sight.

The hedge near which I stopped for a view of the birds was so tall and twiggy it might have been grown for service in a maze. Added to difficulties of visibility was the unfriendly weather. The gentle downpour of an hour before had become a monsoon shower, almost as dense as water from a hosepipe.

I lowered a side window of the car for a few inches so as to use the binoculars. It was an unsatisfactory arrangement. Either the lenses became spattered with rain or they steamed up with the humidity in the car, a dilemma that has brought many raw oaths from the lips of ornithologists with something out of the ordinary to watch. My observations were restricted to short periods, the rest of the time being spent cleaning the lenses.

Two fields away was a large assembly of pink-footed geese, only exceeded in number in my experience by the thousands of birds seen on the Solway marshes. Birds reared on the Thorsaver oasis in central Iceland had now adapted themselves to the equally quiet conditions of rural Scotland. A preference for certain winter quarters continues to express itself from year to year as the older, more experienced geese direct the youngsters to those places offering the best food and sanctuary. It is acquired knowledge, passed on from generation to generation.

The sky became three tones lighter, as the storm abated. I approached the goose flock from another direction, but first I conversed with a helpful farmer—who, incidentally, no longer noticed the birds, though there might be up to 3,000 on his land!

He saw the first of the pinkfeet arrive during the third week in September. In foggy conditions young birds might collide with the electricity wires, cutting off power to the farm. Generally the geese did not turn up to graze in foggy weather; they stayed in clear conditions on the hill. He had known geese arrive at dusk and remain in the fields during the whole of a moonlit night.

The Icelandic origin of many of the geese had been established with the help of experiments undertaken near Dunning. Naturalists laid out nets and shot the nets over parties of grazing geese by rocket power. The captive geese were examined and then released. Details on any foot rings had been noted and rings attached to the legs of any birds that had not previously been handled by man.

The farmer had adapted his routine to the geese in one respect —he no longer planted winter wheat. The land on which they fed was mainly gravelly, with a light loam. Grass was sown as part of the usual crop rotation.

A small acreage given over to growing potatoes was not seriously affected by the geese. The planting of spuds ended just before the birds left the area, and by the time they returned the crop had been lifted. The geese tidied up the fields by eating a few frosted potatoes that remained out.

No great harm is done to established grass—and the birds leave a bonus in the form of a liberal covering of manure. It is arguable that by trimming down winter wheat during a mild winter the geese ensure that there is less damage to the crop in any frosty spell that follows.

With an idea that the geese would accept the car as something impersonal I asked the farmer if I could drive across one of the drier fields. I had been impressed when he told me that he was accepted by the birds as he went about his daily round. Even the sheepdogs were tolerated by the geese providing they did not run directly at the assembled birds.

When my car breasted a ridge, I looked down on to about one thousand grey geese, spread over sections of two large fields, where most of the birds were shearing grass. Within moments the delicate early warning system of the goose flock was operating. Dozens, then hundreds, of heads bobbed up into full view. The birds waddled into positions for mass take-off.

The first birds to become airborne cruised over the solemn grey ranks of indecisive geese. Other groups followed. Then great and wavering lines of geese rose and began to ascend in broad spirals until the whole district appeared to be canopied by grey feathers. The flock, attaining height, drifted eastwards to be concealed from my gaze by the mist. I heard the geese talking long after they had gone from sight.

Next day I motored from Perth to Leven, a loch between the firths of Tay and Forth. Leven occupies a depression scooped out as an incidental in the Pleistocene period, when glaciers swept the scene. It extends to over 3,300 acres—a considerable stretch of loch by lowland standards. Here, in a part of Scotland that many holiday visitors miss because they are inclined to 'write it off to industry' was an area noted for its wildfowl. Kinross, the nearest place, had kept faith with its old spirit of a country town and was quiet. Through traffic had been filtered away by a new motorway.

Loch Leven is large but not deep, averaging about 13 feet, with two 'deeps' that have been plumbed at over eighty feet. Wind frequently ruffles its surface, and my first clear view of it came when white-capped waves were surging to destruction against Leven's several islands. Was it worth-while looking along the shore for stranded fish? There is an account dating to the early part of the eighteenth century that a gale scattered perch and pike along the shoreline and that exultant local people filled carts with fish, selling them at a penny a hundred.

Grey geese plane down to Loch Leven in autumn. Geese were listed in the *Statistical Account* of 1793 along with heron, bittern, snipe, teal, water rail, "king's fisher", coot, swan and gull. The pinkfeet are the first of the grey geese to arrive. Up to twelve thousand have been seen here, some resting, some feeding, some staying and others moving on, so that by midwinter there might be about four thousand geese in the area. Greylags arrive about a fortnight after the pinkfeet. Herds of melodious whooper swans touch down on Leven, having flown the 700-mile course from Iceland that is taken by many of the geese.

A shallow loch, containing nutritious plant and insect food, is very suitable as a feeding ground for ducks. Leven attracts several species: tufted, mallard, wigeon, teal and (in smaller numbers) goldeneye and gadwall. We know a great deal about them from the copious records. Loch Leven is a national nature reserve and also, in part, one of the sanctuaries of the Royal Society for the Protection of Birds.

The R.S.P.B. purchased Vane Farm (300 acres) in 1967. The buildings have their back to Vane Hill but face out over the loch, being approached by a public road that runs amiably between hedges and near fields which, after heavy rain, now glinted with floodwater.

It was a grey day—and cold. Shaggy black cattle grazed or lay ruminating on the pastureland sloping from the road to the edge of the loch. The small rafts of duck were well-scattered, riding rough water or, in the case of goldeneye, diving repeatedly. The low bulk of St Serf's was frilled by white. Grey geese roost on the water not far from this island.

Lapwings stood primly in the fields, waiting for spring. Flocks of starlings fed voraciously, with the quick movements of waders. Oystercatchers made a noisy retreat. When the shock waves of my intrusion appeared to abate I became aware of a flock of two hundred greylags in a field quite close to the road, not very far from the huddle of buildings that is Vane Farm.

The geese could not contain their excitement further. The birds rose in gabbling waves, quickly gaining altitude, splitting into several groups, taking up line or chevron formations, and seeming to occupy a quarter of the sky. Two main flocks were formed, one of which alighted on ploughland a quarter of a mile from the road. It was hard to separate a view of them from the chocolate-brown of freshly-turned earth. The other group, settled in a roadside field, held 104 birds.

There was a sequel to my Perthshire goose-watching. Weeks later I spent a night at Pitlochry, awakening at 5.30 a.m., as the sun's gaze fell on the hilltops across the valley. I walked down to Lake Faskally, having the world to myself.

Faskally appeared to be steaming after a frosty night. The vapour slowly cleared and the water coloured as sunlight struck further down the hills. The conifer plantations were reflected as blotches of green. Highlights of gold and copper could be easily matched up with those sections of hill where dead bracken lay.

The voices of the local greylags rang across rock-girt Faskally as though in an echo-chamber. Then other goose voices were heard. A skein of pinkfeet passed over, travelling to the north, moving lower than the hill summits. The point of the chevron formation had been blunted as birds settled some minor problem of leadership, or perhaps exchanged duties. Ten minutes later another skein of pinkfeet was sweeping by. Were these some of the birds I had seen in Perthshire?

Crossing the footbridge, I gained the public road west of Faskally. Two greylags erupted from the rough ground beyond and, calling loudly, passed over me at a height of only twenty feet. I watched the geese wiffling during a descent to the lake. They alighted, and one goose—presumably the gander—drove off another greylag.

It was almost spring.

INDEX